KU-651-226

Northern Ireland – a problem to every solution

Denis Barritt

Quaker Peace & Service
Northern Friends Peace Board

ISBN 0 901 689 17 3
© 1982

Published by Quaker Peace & Service,
Friends House, Euston Road, London NW1 2BJ
in association with Northern Friends Peace Board,
1 The Grange, Hall Lane, Horsforth, Leeds LS18 5EH

Printed in England by Headley Brothers Ltd.,
109 Kingsway, London WC2B 6PX and Ashford, Kent

This book is published as a contribution to the discussion of the future of Northern Ireland. The views expressed are those of the author.

Contents

Edinburgh Peace and Justice Education Centre Library

St John's Church, Princes Street, Edinburgh
EH2 4BJ

Please return by the following date either to the Centre or to the Quaker Meeting House, 7 Victoria Terrace, Edinburgh (in an addressed envelope, please)

Foreword

It is with great pleasure and satisfaction that I have accepted to write this foreword to a very useful book on Northern Ireland. With pleasure because I regard Denis Barritt as a good personal friend; on my fairly frequent visits to Belfast during the early seventies, Denis and Monica Barritt invariably extended warm hospitality to me and generously shared with me their deep insights into the prevailing situation. Denis Barritt was for 17 years the secretary of the Belfast Council of Social Welfare. That post and a host of 'spare time' activities kept him extremely busy. He retired in August 1980, and immediately he acceded to the request of Quakers and wrote this book.

Satisfaction also, because of a profound interest in and concern for the people of Northern Ireland. To a limited extent this is because it is part of my job to know something of the situation there, but two other, more personal, factors are of much greater importance. I, too, am a Celt, and my background is essentially working-class. It is the members of the working class (the term has greater validity in Northern Ireland than it does on this side of the water these days) who have borne the brunt of the suffering during the present troubles. Taking an oversimplified view of the situation, I have always deeply regretted that the inhabitants of the Shankill and the Falls have concentrated on the 'wrong' issues and, by default, have allowed atrocious social conditions to be perpetuated.

Some readers may be puzzled that a religious society should be interested in Northern Ireland to the extent of commissioning and publishing a book on the subject. A brief explanation may thus be appropriate. Soon after the Society of Friends (Quakers) came into being—over three hundred years ago and at a time of civil war in England—it issued a declaration which reads, in part, '. . . we certainly know, and testify to the world, that the Spirit of Christ, which leads us into all truth, will never move us to fight and war against any man with outward weapons, neither for the kingdom of Christ, nor for the kingdoms of the world.' The great majority of Quakers in Britain and Ireland have steadfastly maintained that position down to the present day.

But, as time passed, other facets of the 'peace testimony' developed: Quakers were not content simply to say 'No' to war. Particularly during the latter half of the nineteenth century and the first half of the twentieth, they were extremely active helping refugees and other victims of war in Europe—indeed, their efforts during the 1939–45 war earned them, jointly with the American Friends Service Committee, the award of the Nobel Peace Prize in 1947. Other matters relating to peace and war have claimed their attention: for instance, again in co-operation with the American Friends Service Committee, they maintain a substantial presence at the United Nations in New York and Geneva. They have also played a small mediating role in a number of situations of open conflict in Africa and Asia during the past few decades.

The situation in Northern Ireland is an international issue in the sense that people on every continent know that it is beset by civil strife. A few years ago I was travelling by train in East Germany, when a local resident questioned me very closely on the subject. He happened to be quite well informed, but so many people—including a lot in Britain—are not. They may well have a wealth of information but, for some reason or other, their views on Northern Ireland are frequently coloured by prejudice. A strong case can be made out for a book which sets out the facts of the situation in a sensitive, objective and disinterested way. This book goes a long way towards fulfilling that need.

In 1969, a Quaker book on Northern Ireland was published under the title of *Orange and Green*. Denis Barritt was the principal author of that, his co-author being Arthur Booth, at that time secretary of the Northern Friends Peace Board. Many copies of *Orange and Green* were sold, and it was translated into French, German and Italian. In one sense, *Northern Ireland—A Problem to Every Solution* is the successor to *Orange and Green*; it deals with events that have occurred since the latter was published. In another sense it is complementary to *Orange and Green*, for the first volume contained a good deal of historical and other background material, a knowledge of which is essential for a proper understanding of the Northern Ireland situation. However, *Orange and Green* is different from *Northern Ireland—A Problem to Every Solution*: the first was the result of four to five years' discussion among Quakers in the Republic of Ireland, Northern Ireland, Scotland and the north of England, whereas the present book is essentially the authorship of Denis Barritt.

While I commend the book as a whole to readers one particular chapter is worthy of especial mention. I refer to the one entitled *Voluntary Reconciling Organisations*. Very many people in Britain and elsewhere in the world have a mental picture of Northern Ireland in which Catholic and Protestant rarely meet and when they do blood is sure to flow. Some years ago in Zimbabwe (then Southern Rhodesia) someone remarked to me in all seriousness that at least the violence there was far less than in Northern

Ireland! At that time large sections of the rural areas of Rhodesia were in turmoil and at least thirty people a day were being killed! I could hardly believe my ears.

It will surely come as a considerable surprise therefore to learn how active many private citizens are in the realm of reconciliation. As far as I am aware, in no other publication does information about the non-governmental organisations appear in such a comprehensive way. Some day the people of Northern Ireland will live in peace and the efforts of the devoted members of these voluntary bodies will have been vindicated.

WALTER MARTIN
Friends House, London
April 1982

Introduction

I have been asked by the Peace Committee of Quaker Peace & Service to review the Northern Ireland situation at a time when a workable formula for the restoration of devolved government is being sought. It was suggested that I should bring up to date books on Northern Ireland, the writing of which I shared with other Friends.

Anyone born in Northern Ireland finds himself trapped by the past and so it was necessary to look back, particularly to establish our varying identities, but I have not attempted to deal in detail with events before 1960. I must refer those unacquainted with the long Home Rule debate, the establishment of the State of Northern Ireland and its operation over its first 40 years or so, to a number of works in the bibliography on page 143. My own interpretation of these years remains as expressed in the *Northern Ireland Problem* (1962) with Charles Carter and with Arthur Booth in *Orange and Green* (1972) for the Northern Friends Peace Board.

The use of the words 'Protestant' and 'Catholic' remain, in my opinion, the clearest way of expressing the main division in the community, but I have used the term 'Loyalist' to distinguish those Protestants who take a more intransigent line than mainstream Unionists. On the Catholic side the word 'Republican' I use for whose who reject the more moderate Nationalist approach. It is from these two sub-divisions that the men and women of violence are mainly drawn, though both terms include those who do not approve of violent methods.

As far as possible I have adopted the Quaker way of referring to people by their Christian and surname, omitting any title. However, it has been convenient to use a title on occasions to indicate a member of the House of Lords, or to designate a church dignitary.

I would like to thank all those who have read all or part of the manuscript and made helpful suggestions, and also those who have given me special permission to quote from their material. In particular I wish to thank Harvey Gillman, of Quaker Peace & Service, and my wife, Monica, for the painstaking way they have helped me improve the text.

1 The peaks and troughs of hope

It would be understandable for anyone to despair of ever finding a way to lasting peace in Northern Ireland. Every move seems to evoke a perverse intransigent response. One could say of the people of Northern Ireland that they can find 'a problem to every solution'.

'Of course, the violence is all part of an international plan', one is told from time to time; 'they' use both sides of the dispute, though just how 'they' operate is always left vague. Anyone who has experienced the depth of vehemence of Irish Nationalism—and where better to find it than in London's Hyde Park or in Boston, Massachusetts—does not need to postulate some international Marxist master-mind to account for the trouble. There is no need to look for external promptings to account for the opposing Protestant 'not-an-inch' resolution. The latter's emotion is slower to come to boiling point, and it owes much to the Scots' influence, which has that 'self-reliance, capacity for hard work, imperviousness to hostile opinion, unflagging determination to defend what they had gained and the peculiar cohesion and discipline that they owed to their Presbyterianism.'[1] This was the spirit which possibly 250,000 Ulster Scots took with them during the eighteenth century to North America. There they made an appreciable mark in the fight against Great Britain for independence and in the governing of the emergent United States. This is the spirit of 'Ulster Nationalism' abroad today, which cries 'no surrender' to Irish Republican Nationalism—and, if necessary, *in extremis*, to their friends in Great Britain also.

From the previous paragraph it might appear that life in Northern Ireland consists of a continual clash between the dour unyielding Orangemen and the Catholic Nationalists, inflamed with bitter emotion. This is simply not the case. It is perhaps surprising how much of normal civilised life remains, not for all, but for so large a proportion of the population. One meets an open friendliness in both communities and in spite of the terrible deeds that have been done, in spite of the terrible acts still taking place, Northern Ireland is by and large a friendly (if not very happy) place in which to live. It is this spirit of humanity which breaks through the bitterness and gives one encouragement to continue to seek for reconciliation.

It is now possible to look back over the past three or four decades with that measure of objectivity which hindsight gives. Some features emerge. Many of the Protestant majority just did not realise the extent to which the Catholic third of the population were made to feel like 'second-class citizens'. Although many Protestant workers were in an advantageous position vis-à-vis their Catholic counterparts they did not by and large regard themselves as being in a privileged position, though probably a number felt they should have been as a reward for their loyalty to the state.[2]

At the end of the sixties, with TV cameras present at the civil rights demonstrations, Great Britain and much of the world 'discovered' Northern Ireland for the first time since 1921. It was then that Catholic disabilities tended to be exaggerated and the Province and its rules likened to apartheid in the Republic of South Africa, which was clearly ridiculous.

The sixties now emerge as a period propitious for reforms and changes which might well have saved the Province from bloodshed. A number of events had combined to bring about this better climate.

The campaign of violence which the IRA had mounted in 1956 to blow up Customs posts, army barracks, police stations and government offices near the border, had lost its momentum and was terminated in 1962. All those who had been interned (187 being the peak number) had been released. The Church had declared that to be a member of the IRA was a 'mortal sin'. This campaign, in contrast to the later one in the seventies, had failed to attract Catholic youth in any number. The Republicans decided to take a political stand and try to bring the Protestant workers with them in a drive for an all-Ireland 32 county Workers' Republic.

The advent of Pope John XXIII introduced a new liberal spirit into the Catholic Church. Following the Vatican Councils the wind of spiritual change was felt even in reactionary Ireland. The Catholic Church presented a new image of co-operation; both clergy and laity were much more willing to come forward to take part in activities in the community which were not specifically 'Catholic'. Active steps were also taken to invite non-Catholics into some Catholic-sponsored organisations.

A new spirit was also creeping into the Protestant churches where resolutions condemning religious discrimination were being passed at annual meetings and synods. In 1965 a member of the Presbyterians' General Assembly called upon his fellow Presbyterians to apologise for their attitudes towards the minority in the past. The next year the General Assembly accepted for discussion a report from one of their commissions which called for removal of a number of Catholic grievances. Not all church members felt this way, in fact the liberal wings of both denominations had more in common with the liberals in other denominations than with their own right wing.

At governmental level, Northern Ireland had in 1963 a new Prime Minister, Terence O'Neill, who had not been a part of the embittering days of the 1921–23 rioting. In October 1964 he said in the Stormont House of Commons: 'My principal aims are . . . to make Northern Ireland economically stronger and more prosperous . . . and to build bridges between the two traditions within our community.' This was the first time that reconciliation had been stated as official policy.

In January 1965 O'Neill invited the Taoiseach (Prime Minister) of the Republic, then Sean Limas, to visit Belfast and shortly afterwards returned the visit. Nationalists in the Stormont parliament saw this more as an honest attempt at reconciliation and their leader, Eddie McAteer, decided for the first time to accept the title of official leader of opposition. A couple of years later, when Lynch had become the Taoiseach, the visits were repeated and passed off almost without comment. But all was not well in O'Neill's parliamentary party. Some back benchers had met together to try to curb their leader's action. While some people felt that O'Neill was dragging his feet over the 'bridge-building' aspects of his policy, the right wing of his party became more and more determined that 'O'Neill must go'. In holding back measures of reform, they did a tragic disservice to Protestants and to the whole Province of Ulster. The time was ripe for change, and a few reasonable acts such as the repeal of at least some of the clauses of the Special Powers Act,[3] a grant in aid for the Catholic maternity hospital in Belfast, a more reasonable points system for the allocation of council houses throughout the Province, would have convinced the Catholic minority that justice was intended. Such reforms were in fact outlined in the Northern Labour Party's document *Labour in the Sixties*. Terence O'Neill unfortunately chose to regard this group as an opposition party, though they supported his programme of reform.

Of course the old fears and tribal shibboleths were all present, but they were quiescent. When Ian Paisley led his flock in a picket of the Presbyterian Assembly, and when in 1964 he led a protest against the Republican Party (representing the illegal Sinn Fein party) who had flown the flag of the Republic, the tricolour, at their Belfast party office, both groups were referred to as 'the lunatic fringe'. So was a shadowy group calling itself the Ulster Volunteer Force (using the name of the former 'establishment' type gun-runners of 1914), and whose members were connected with the murder of two Catholics during the summer of 1966. Soon this group was to be declared an illegal organisation under the Special Powers Act. It did not go unnoticed that this was the first time that act had been used against a 'Protestant' group.

There was no thought of ending the devolved rule of the Northern Ireland Parliament. This was not a serious practical possibility. For most Catholics, Irish unity was an ideal to be hoped for at some future determined date—without, they hoped, the loss of the better social security benefits obtainable in the North.

All was not lost. In 1968, International Human Rights Year, a civil rights movement was formed whose demonstrations remained non-violent. If there was violence, it was the police who provided it when breaking up the Londonderry Civil Rights demonstration on 5 October 1968, an event which had the effect of opening the problems of Northern Ireland's divided community to Great Britain and to the world. After only five weeks of demonstrations O'Neill was able to announce a package deal of reforms.[4]

This was the time for the demonstrators to leave the streets to consolidate these considerable gains. No life had been lost although an unwarranted Protestant attack on a march of student demonstrators from Belfast to Londonderry in January 1969 came dangerously near to so doing. The civil rights movement, having tasted success, was in no mood to sit back and leave the Unionist Government in peace. Ian Paisley had been rallying Protestants to stage counter-demonstrations. Emotions built up and as is noted in Chapter 4 violence broke out in August 1969 and the first lives were lost. The army was called on to the streets to aid the Royal Ulster Constabulary and soon to take riot control out of their hands.

To those in Northern Ireland trying to promote reconciliation, these days were a worrying and frustrating time. If the violence of the years ahead could have been fully foreseen it would have been a time of utter despair. To the dispassionate outsider the period made an interesting study of the problems of change in a static society. In Northern Ireland the Unionist Party has been in power for almost fifty years. Superficially conditions are relatively peaceful, economically they are improving. Thus why change, why stir up and encourage your traditional enemies? In many of the minority, who harbour grievances, having had no effective political voice for half a century, resentment builds up until measures which once would have given satisfaction, if they had been freely granted, are now seen to be too little and too late.

The status quo element then says to their liberal reform wing, 'What did we tell you; you give these people an inch and they at once ask for a yard.' In many cases the situation is complicated by the fact that some members of the 'out' group become apathetic over a period and only clamour for reforms when it appears that change is a practical proposition. The real danger occurs, however, when violence breaks out, because this allows the right wing to claim with greater vehemence, 'If you had listened to us there would have been no loss of life, this was a peaceful place until you stirred up this lot.' Reactionary measures may then be applied or, if it is a case of two or more contending factions, all sides feel they have a just cause for violent retaliation, the original issues become confused and, as in overt war, truth is an early casualty. Violence is often met with violence, but eventually the inherent goodness of human beings prevails. The timetable however is a long one.

The split in the IRA which took place in Dublin in January 1969 and which is dealt with in Chapter 4, passed almost unnoticed at the time but was to have a terrible effect on life in Northern Ireland. Apart from material destruction and the deaths, directly or indirectly, of over 2,000 people, the Provisional IRA's campaign led to the disastrous response by the Unionist Government in re-introducing internment without trial, and finally to the proroguing of the Northern Ireland Government.

If the ending of the Stormont Government is looked upon as a 'success' for violence, it should be pointed out that the thing that all parties (except the Republicans) agreed about is that there should be some form of devolved government of Northern Ireland.

It should be noted that the numerous social and political reforms in Northern Ireland, from 1968 and the ensuing years, had all been enacted, or at least agreed upon before the Provisional IRA commenced their campaign. These new features which are regarded as beneficial have come about in spite of, and not because of, the IRA.

In spite of the violence there was to be another period of hope—the 1974 Assembly, Northern Ireland's own devolved government once again proving, at least for the short period it was allowed to exist, that a coalition with the minority party could work. The misguided efforts of the Loyalists in bringing down this government by means of the Ulster Workers' Strike is dealt with in some detail in Chapter 3.

There have been therefore glimpses of hope, practical examples of how it may be possible to get beyond the divide. There was the climate of change in the sixties bringing co-operation across the divide and opening the doors to constructive change in a way which was not believed possible a few years earlier. There was the example of the Power-Sharing Executive in the Assembly of 1974, and the emergence and growth of the Alliance Party built on shared leadership within its ranks. This Party suffered a set-back along with other liberal groups with the increasing polarisation following the deaths of the ten hunger strikers, but in the past emotions have been raised and have gradually settled again. There have been various spontaneous outbursts of a desire for peace among the rank and file of Northern Ireland's people, notably the large rallies organised by the Peace People during the latter half of 1976. Even during the summer of 1981 in the wake of the hunger strike and the alarming manifestations of Protestant frustration, and following the murder of Robert Bradford MP, the fact that a priest was given a standing ovation in his church in Strabane for his open condemnation of the Provisional IRA was a straw in the wind of hope. There remains the continued commitment of members of a number of reconciling movements whose story is told in Chapter 6.

The strongest potential reconciling agency of all must remain the Christian Church. Mention has been made of the churches' contribution to the improvement of group relations in the sixties; it is sad that the action of the Church does not appear more frequently in the ensuing text, for after all, it is not a question of different religions coming together, but merely denominations of the one Christian Church whose members were exhorted from the beginning to 'keep the unity of the Spirit in the bond of Peace'.

The church denominations have been trapped by their past history as much as any groupings of peoples in the island of Ireland. They were indeed a major part of the division. The very dedicated nature of the faith of many to their own particular approach has made any ecumenical advance appear as a move to tolerate something less than the truth.

The Catholic insistence, prior to the Vatican Councils, that the beliefs of the 'separated brethren' were heretical, placed Protestants in the position of being 'second-class Christians', whose response was to regard many Catholic teachings to be in error and to be shunned at all costs. The Orange Order, it should be remembered, was formed to resist the practices of the Church of Rome but to 'refrain from all uncharitable words, actions or sentiments towards his Roman Catholic brethren'.[5] Many would regard this exhortation more honoured in the breach, though some Protestants still join the Order as part of their religious duty and each Lodge will have its own Chaplain.

Opposition to Catholic theology merely reinforced the tribal mores and strengthened the political belief that the Catholic Church was a vast monolithic structure, organised from Rome, to take over Northern Ireland and deprive Protestants of their birthright of freedom of worship and to jeopardise their material livelihood. To Catholics the Church was their unifying influence dating back to Penal Law days and the great campaigns of Daniel O'Connell in the early years of the last century for the right of Catholics to enter Parliament and for a repeal of the Act of 1800 which did away with the Dublin Parliament.

It is curious how fearful both sides were of coming together lest this should weaken their members' faith, when one would have thought that it might have been an opportunity to witness to the 'truth'. There was also the more understandable fear of mixed marriages, which, in such a divided society, did place a very real social strain on such a union.

Unfortunately, so many ardent souls have concentrated on the soul salvation aspect when what is required is whole salvation and the translation of the undoubted sincerity of faith into social and political actions. It is remarkable how the minutes of church meetings, even during times of tribal clashes, reveal a religious body singularly unconcerned about the violence and its causes, but stirred up because a place of recreation was to be opened on a Sunday.

It takes a strong-willed cleric to tell his congregation unpalatable truths which concern them and cannot be blamed on some other group. Some who have seen the light have refrained from speaking out lest they split their congregation in half, an understandable, but in the long run, self-defeating rationalisation.

In the chapter on reconciling organisations reference is made to the changes in church attitudes—to the growth, for instance, of the Irish Council of Churches (still viewed with suspicion by a number of congregations) and the co-operation of the Roman Catholic Church with the Irish hierarchy. The outcome has been a number of joint conferences held in a hotel at Ballymascanlon, just across the border near Dundalk. A number of joint studies have been commissioned on various problems such as drug abuse, housing, teenage drinking, and with particular relevance, 'Violence in Ireland'. The report of this study was published in 1977 as a paperback.[6] The Joint Working Party quite unequivocally condemns all campaigns of violence and killing and recommends that the churches actively support peace and reconciling movements.

Although ecumenism may still be a dirty word, particularly in some Protestant churches (where it is feared that it will lead to a takeover by the Catholic Church) there is much more co-operation and the holding of joint prayer groups and services are no longer 'news'. So often one stops to think 'this could not have taken place fifteen years ago'.

It would be sad if the increased co-operation were to coincide with a decline in the churches' influence. Some years back a Presbyterian cleric in Dublin maintained he would never be given a parking ticket; he basked in the deference shown to his Catholic brothers! It is doubtful whether the churches could claim the same immunity today. A short while ago a group of rioting youths could be dispelled by the parish priest; today they would be more likely to tell him in no uncertain terms where he could go. And no-one could have made a stronger condemnation of violence than did Pope John Paul on the occasion of his visit to the Republic of Ireland in the summer of 1979.[7] The violence however continued unabated.

The strong statement of Cardinal O'Fiaich in November 1981, condemning violence carried out by any paramilitary organisation as a 'mortal sin' is to be welcomed, as was the influence of Father Denis Faul in encouraging the parents of the remaining hunger strikers to call for medical intervention to end this sad waste of life.

Church adherence, however, in Northern Ireland, remains stronger than in most West European countries. The members have therefore a great challenge and a great opportunity to take Northern Ireland beyond the divide.

The current situation is fluid. It would be of no value to try to suggest what will happen. Various hopeful ways ahead can be seen, but they will have to be chosen according to the opportunities as they present themselves. Thus this introduction must also serve as a conclusion.

To try to evaluate positive moves, one needs to look at basic group divisions and their interaction over the years. Hence the first thing to ask is, who the people in Northern Ireland are and what has been happening at government level. The next question to ask is how a state copes with violence in society or what happens to law and order. Northern Ireland is a place where people go on living, but one needs to ask how the violence affects their day to day lives and how the state services function against this pattern of violence, where the economic situation and the very high level of unemployment present problems enough on their own. After that it is useful to have a look at some suggestions as to the future of the Province and its relations with Great Britain and the Republic.

Not much has been written about the work of the various reconciling organisations (apart from the Peace People for a time) whose solid day to day work towards sanity is largely ignored by the television cameras. It is impossible to evaluate the extent of their influence but their contribution is certainly worth looking at, as is done in Chapter 6. With the churches these reconciling organisations could have a significant role in building a state where co-operation to reduce unemployment and build a better life for all in the Province replaces division.

2 A case of identity: who are the people of Northern Ireland?

In a variety of ways the historical development of the North of Ireland has differed from that of the rest of the island. Professor Estyn Evans, from a life-long study of its physical and cultural history, has advanced the theory that the reason for the difference perhaps 'lies in the soil' and that we should look for an ecological rather than a purely political or religious answer. Be that as it may, it was in the North that the original inhabitants dating back into the mists of time, held out longest against the Gaels whose invasions from Gaul commenced in the first century B.C.

Again it was in the North that the ancient Irish Earldoms held out longest against the forces of Elizabeth in the sixteenth century. Their final defeat came soon after her death when James I made generous enough conditions for both the Earls of Tyrone and of Tyrconnell, allowing them to live on their lands. However, they felt that the only thing left of the ancient Gaelic laws and culture was the Gaelic tongue, and the two secretly set sail from Lough Swilly near Londonderry in 1607 with many of their retainers for an unknown continental destination.

The Crown declared this an act of treason—the Earls, it was claimed, had left to raise an army of invasion—and seized their extensive lands. Those considered loyal to the Crown, Anglicans from the North of England and Presbyterians from Scotland, were invited to come as 'undertakers' to settle and work the land. These 'Planters', as they came to be known, were not supposed to employ the native Irish, but because of shortage of labour did in fact do so. Earlier settlers from England, coming mostly to the south of the island, had inter-married with the native Irish, adopted their language and become 'more Irish than the Irish themselves'. In the sixteenth century with the Reformation these planters became Protestants, but the indigenous Irish remained in the original church and were loyal to Rome. This was the foundation of the Ulster we know today, for there was very little inter-marriage, and the new settlers never used the Irish language. You could, at that time, tell the groups apart by dress and by tongue. Vestiges remain today in the names of streets in some provincial northern towns; English Street, Scotch Street, and Irish Street can still be seen.

Another difference between the North and the South was that whereas the later settlers in the South were largely members of the professions or landed gentry, in the North the planters were often artisans reinforced by others who came from the north of England and Scotland and formed a cross-section of the economic spectrum. There was never any thought at this time of Ireland being ruled by the Catholic Irish, so that Protestants, including those living in the nine counties of the ancient Province of Ulster, were contented enough to be known as 'Irish'.[1]

During the last 20 years of the eighteenth century, the leader of the Irish Parliament in Dublin, Henry Grattan, was able to gain an increased measure of autonomy and to claim, 'Ireland is now a nation,' yet it was a 100% Protestant Parliament. Catholics did not even gain the right to vote until 1793, but it was not until the triumph of the great Irish leader Daniel O'Connell in 1829 that Catholics, and incidentally O'Connell himself, were permitted to take a seat in Parliament.

Much had happened in these intervening years including the French Revolution. The ideals of the French revolutionary leaders had a strong influence on sections of the Irish people, particularly on the liberal wing of the Presbyterian denomination in the North. A number of these formed the Society of United Irishmen who stood for complete Irish independence to be coupled with radical reforms within Ireland. In the rest of Ireland supporters were largely drawn from the Catholic community but led by the Dublin Protestant, Wolfe Tone. Catholic supporters of the United Irishmen were more interested in obtaining the land confiscated from them under the Penal Laws, than in the ideals of 'Liberté, Egalité, Fraternité'—but Presbyterian United Irishmen saw themselves as liberating their Catholic brothers from all vestige of the Penal Laws.

This is remembered in some Nationalist and Republican thinking in the South of Ireland today, and among expatriate Irishmen, but to think that this still exists is wishful thinking. It must be remembered, however, that not all Protestants in the North felt this way. Many looked upon these United Irishmen as 'rebels' particularly as they became a secret society and resorted to violence in 1798—'the '98 Rebellion'.

Also at this time, 1795, the Orange Order was born. It came as a result of a skirmish between a Protestant Loyalist and a Catholic faction at the town of Dungannon. This secret society formed 'to maintain the laws of peace of the country and the Protestant constitution' had a chequered existence until it emerged as the main rallying force of the Protestant community. At the time of the '98 Rebellion it played its part in helping the forces of the Crown, not all that strong, to quell the rising.

The final outcome was the abolition of the Irish Parliament by the Act of Union in 1800 which transferred all Irish representation to Westminster. A number of Protestants were against this loss of local power. Indeed the Lord Lieutenant and the officers of the Crown had to resort to bribery to gain a majority in the Irish House of Commons in favour of the transfer.

Some vestiges of liberal Presbyterianism outlasted the failure of the rebellion, but as a force in the land it evaporated surprisingly quickly. One reason is to be found in the success of Daniel O'Connell in his mass non-violent campaign for the right of Catholics to take their seats at Westminster. He followed this campaign with one for the repeal of the Union. Even though unsuccessful he was able to command a huge following. This united for the first time the mass of Catholics campaigning for the ending of the Penal Laws and brought into being the Nationalist concept of an independent Ireland. O'Connell was not in fact calling for a republic with a complete break with the Crown, but it was clear that any future Irish government would not be dominated by Protestants. It is worthy of note that when O'Connell was holding vast meetings in favour of the repeal of the Act of Union he came north to Ulster in 1843 expecting to meet with the liberal Presbyterian spirit which had provided the leaders in the '98 Rebellion. He met, however, with violent opposition and had to leave the Province in a hurry never to return.

Irish Nationalist sentiment became more insistent, especially among the bitter expatriate Irish in America. The Fenian movement was formed and Northern Protestants began to see the threat of Home Rule actually materialising.

It was Britain's failure to cope adequately with the terrible potato famine of 1845 and the following years that was the chief cause of this bitterness. The population of Ireland fell from about 8½ million in 1845 to 6½ million in 1851. No one knows the exact number but probably about one million died of malnutrition and the consequent epidemic. About the same number emigrated—and the process continued so that the population in 1911 was 4,380,219. However, the terrible effects of the potato crop failures were to some degree mitigated in the North by the cottage textile industry, providing the population, rural as well as urban, with an alternative income allowing the people to purchase food. By the eighteen forties there were spinning and weaving factories in a number of towns. A short-lived cotton industry had opened the way to this new development which then gave place to linen from about 1835.

Thus although the Ulster workhouses were crowded with an influx from the poorer farms and especially from the counties 'west of the Bann'—bringing with them the dreaded famine fever, dysentery and typhus—conditions in the north-east were not nearly as bad as in the rest of the island. By July 1847 it was estimated that over three million persons in Ireland were receiving soup from Poor Law union kitchens (made mainly from the maize imported from North America by Sir Robert Peel for the purpose). It was only the unions of Antrim, Belfast, and Newtownards which did not see the need for the soup-kitchen scheme.

Therefore in the North there was not the same bitterness against the English for their seeming indifference to the famine and its consequences. The lot of the Northern farmer was also made more tolerable by the universal custom of allowing the tenant to benefit from any capital he had spent on his property. If the landlord wanted to secure the land he had to pay the tenant for the improvements. In the South so many of the landlords were Protestants who did not live near their Catholic tenants. Sometimes they did not, at least for long periods, even live in Ireland. Rents could be pushed up and if the tenant did not pay he was evicted. The Northern landlord usually knew his tenants, he probably met them at church on Sunday or they might well both be Orange brethren attending the same Lodge meeting. Thus there was not the bitter agrarian discontent, as in the South. Though the landlord lived in 'the big house', he was an Ulsterman as they were. Even though the Catholic could claim he was pushed off 'into the bog', or on to poor 'mountainy' land, nevertheless he still benefited from the Ulster Tenant Custom like everyone else.

During the second half of the last century Belfast grew rapidly and the economic links with Great Britain were cemented. The population of Belfast was 37,000 in 1821, and had risen to 100,000 by the turn of the half century. By 1881 it had doubled and by 1901 it had reached 349,000. This growth was due to the expanding trade in linen, shipbuilding, textile machinery and later rope making and tobacco. Many of the industrial leaders had come from England and Scotland. Towards the end of the eighteenth century the Barbour family set up a branch of their Scottish linen thread business near Lisburn. The cotton industry was started by a Lancashire textile printer, Nicholas Grimshaw; power-driven spinning, first cotton and then linen, was due to the initiative of John Hind of Manchester. The most noted industrialist was a Yorkshireman, Edward Harland, who founded what was to become the largest single shipbuilding firm in the world.

Ireland has no coal worthy of the name—nor any iron ore. Thus links with the coal and iron ore fields of Scotland, England and Wales were required to provide the raw materials for industry and the fast expanding population of Great Britain formed the chief market for the manufactured items.

As the rest of Ireland did not have anything like this industrial growth the development of the social and cultural life of the people would have been different even without any religious influence. Some would argue that this industrial growth would not have happened apart from the large input of Anglicans from the North of England and Scottish Presbyterians which took place in the plantations from 1607 onwards and gave north-east Ireland a different temperament, outlook and identity.

The Tithe Act of 1838 went some of the way to stop the practice of the Established Church from taking, in kind, one tenth of the farmers' produce annually—from which dissenters suffered alongside Catholics—and the whole objectionable process was ended in 1869 with the disestablishment of the Anglican Church in Ireland. A barrier between the Presbyterians and the Church of Ireland was thus weakened at this time.

In the meantime a spell-binding orator in the O'Connell mould appeared in the ranks of the Presbyterians. Henry Cooke was a fundamentalist evangelical minister with a large following who called for a strict application of the Westminster Confession of Faith for all entering the Presbyterian ministry. This outmoded and objectionable anti-Catholic document had been in the main allowed to lapse—positively so—by a group within the Presbyterian Synod who were known as the New Lighters. When the conservatives gained the upper hand the New Lighters withdrew in 1830 to become at a later date the Non-Subscribing Presbyterian Church which in Northern Ireland includes those who are Unitarians.

Henry Cooke's preaching also strengthened the maintenance of the union with Britain, as a protection from the Catholic Irish nation and drew the dissenters closer to the Anglicans. Indirectly the trend was reinforced by an evangelical revival which swept across the Province of Ulster in 1859—an influence which was still felt 100 years later. The strong emphasis on soul salvation deflected otherwise dedicated people from the positive social and political reform emphasis in nonconformist branches of the Church in Britain. The Government of Northern Ireland, it was argued, gave protection for the proclamation of the evangelical Christian message, so that nothing should be done to weaken the position of the Unionist Government and perhaps open the doors to the 'errors' of Roman Catholicism.

Home Rule agitation and the eventual passing of the Home Rule Bill in 1914 closed the Protestant ranks which were firmly sealed by the opposition to the common German enemy from 1914 to 1918.

The decision of the six Northern counties to opt out of rule from Dublin under the Government of Ireland Act of 1920 and the formation of the devolved Northern Ireland state did not solve the Northern Protestants' identity problem; to some extent it intensified it. The Unionists had not wanted partition. With Sir Edward Carson, they wished to preserve Westminster rule for the whole land. Devolved self-rule for the North was second best and so Unionists did not celebrate their self-rule for Ulster with any outburst of patriotic fervour. The continuation of Republican violence against partition which lasted for almost two years, and the fact that none of the 'Catholic' opposition (six Nationalist and six Sinn Fein seats out of 52) took their seats in the first Northern Ireland parliament did not encourage the Unionist Government to feel that they were required to establish a regime acceptable to the Nationalist minority even though this amounted to a third of the population. Seen from the vantage point of half a century later, one realises how unfortunate it was that the Unionist Government did not take more positive steps to build up a stronger sense of national identity for the Province, one in which some Catholics at least might share. They were always content to say, 'We are British', bringing out the spectre of Irish Unity and Home Rule before each election, or at any time when opposition to their rule, on the Protestant side, might lead to the formation of a splinter Protestant party. So the Northern citizens could still call themselves Irish if they wished but the Protestant would add, 'We are the loyal Irish' to which the Catholic would retort, 'Loyal to what—a foreign monarch? We are the Irish loyalists, loyal to Ireland.'

As the life of Northern Ireland became stabilised and secure, particularly after it became clear that the 1925 Border Commission was not going to recommend dismembering the northern territory, a local 'Northern Ireland' pride did begin to develop. Statements were made beginning, 'We, in Ulster . . .' and usually this meant Protestant Ulster and the Catholic community was all too often ignored. It suited the Unionist Government to leave all Catholics as 'the opposition' and not to try to win their support. This would not have been an impossible task for Catholics are Northerners also and often feel themselves different from their co-religionists in the South. True, they would feel happier with the ancient nine county province of Ulster rather than the Unionist-dominated six county Northern Ireland. There was a period during the Home Rule debates when the Northern Ireland representatives looked at the possibility of self-government for the whole Province of Ulster, but this would have given only a 54% Protestant overall majority and so they settled for the 66%/34% balance of the present Northern Ireland—much to the chagrin of the pockets of Loyalists living in counties Donegal, Monaghan and Cavan.

The Ulster Protestant, particularly the Presbyterian, has a soft spot in his heart for the Scot. On a clear day from the Antrim cliffs, one can see the houses at Port Patrick 22 miles across the Irish Sea. Before the coming of the railway it was easier to set sail for Scotland than to go to Dublin by the roads then in existence. Many Scots had come from the Ayrshire coast to settle in Co. Antrim. The Sassenach could easily be misled by the characteristic Ballymena accent into thinking it was a Scots community. However, the Ulster Protestants are not Scots — and if they are more British than the English they certainly are not English. There is a love/hate relationship with those in England. The great men in all walks of life learnt about in British history—and it is British history learnt in non-Catholic schools, not Irish history—are revered and vicarious pride is shared.

Northern Ireland's population is about one fortieth of that of the British Isles and its area about equal to that of Yorkshire. The sea boundary and the existence of a separate Parliament does give the Ulster person something of a separate identity as compared with, for example, the man from Cornwall or the Tyneside Geordie. It is quite unreasonable to expect Northern Ireland to compete with the rest of the United Kingdom in every walk of life—and yet so often the Ulster Protestant has felt placed in an inferior position vis-à-vis his English neighbour. So when the English person in Ulster voices a criticism of life in the Province, as he would do quite naturally in any other part of Great Britain, it is taken as a national slight and an inference that the English person feels superior.

Unskilled labour one recruits from the near neighbourhood, for the top positions one throws the net wider. If an advertisement covers the British Isles, the expectancy is that the best applicants would not always be from 'home'. Many from Ulster—and this includes Catholics as well as Protestants—hold leading positions in industry, in the professions, arts and in the church in the rest of the UK. They seem to merge with the local scene, while in Northern Ireland, the person from England, Wales or Scotland appears to stand out and at times to evoke the feeling, 'Do they never appoint an Ulsterman?' However, the Englishman who is understanding of this attitude and shows that he appreciates the attributes of Ulster, its land and its people, of whom he is happy to be a part, is soon accepted and finds Northern Ireland a very friendly and pleasant place in which to live—even during times of civil disturbance.

It is an irritation, to the Protestant at any rate, to hear an outsider say, 'Oh—you Irish'—almost as annoying as to be asked during the Stormont days—'Do I have to go through the Customs to go to Belfast?' A woman from England moved recently to East Belfast to offer service to the local community. When speaking to a local group, mostly of young people, she found considerable initial hostility. She persevered, however, and won acceptance for what she was proposing for the area. When she asked what had been wrong at the start, she was told, 'You said it was good to be in Ireland: this is Ulster, not Ireland.'

People in the rest of the UK now know more about Northern Ireland owing, sadly, to the reporting of violent activities on television, radio and the press. Almost inevitably the impression is given of continuous ubiquitous bombing and murder. The Ulsterman can be forgiven the wry smile when his host on leaving him at Heathrow for the Belfast shuttle remarks that he would like to come and visit him in Northern Ireland, 'when it is safe again to go.' It's an ill wind . . . it is now possible for an Ulster comedian to be understood at least in parts of Britain and for plays about conditions in Northern Ireland to be appreciated in the rest of the UK.

It is difficult to give an estimate of how people feel about their identity or for that matter about an attitude to an event. But this is not without importance and can give an indication of how a peaceful society may be achieved.

Numbers are misleading. One can gather into a hall quite a sizeable group, enthusiastic about a certain way of life or political approach and be tempted to extrapolate much too optimistically. Supporters may have attended in good numbers but be drawn from only a tiny minority of the population.

Short of overburdening the census return form with numerous mandatory questions which would puzzle many citizens, one turns to the carefully weighted sample surveys. Professor Richard Rose of Strathclyde University conducted a searching attitude survey in Northern Ireland in 1967. The response to a relevant question, 'Which of these terms describe the way you usually think of yourself' is given in Appendix B. It will be seen that at least one-fifth of the Catholic population look upon themselves as being British or Ulstermen. It is also interesting that a fifth of Protestants questioned think of themselves first of all as Irish.

It is now possible to compare this pre-violence survey with one conducted in May 1979 by E. P. Moxon-Browne of the Department of Political Science, Queen's University (see also Appendix B). Some of the questions were chosen to give a comparison with Professor Rose's questions after ten years of violent confrontation. It will be seen that the Catholic responses showed a marked similarity with the earlier survey and that 20% of their number still feel themselves to be British or Ulstermen. The percentage of Protestants thinking of themselves as Irish fell considerably from 20% to 7.8% and those forsaking the title of Ulsterman in favour of straightforward British were appreciable, the Ulster title falling from 32% to 19.8%. Mr. Moxon-Browne points out that when breaking down the responses by socio-economic rankings, those Protestants in the unskilled labouring class were more inclined to call themselves Ulstermen (45.2%) rather than British and of the Catholics a smaller proportion of unskilled workers (only 10.7%) considered themselves to be British.

For the Peace People, Ciaran McKeown steadfastly used the term the 'Northern Irish people' to try to establish an acceptable identity which could be shared by Protestant and Catholic alike.[2] Catholics would not feel excluded by the use of the word 'Irish' but would have to accept the reality of the situation that they were Northern and separate from the South. The Protestant could receive his assurance that 'Northern Irish' did not mean a united Ireland but that he must accept the reality of the Irish culture and influence.

Each new spate of violence increases the polarising feeling of belonging to separate communities and re-awakens tribal fears and frustrations which makes further violence more likely. The men who are fanatically conscious of their national identity are given more power, those at the reconciling centre tend to wield less influence. There are a few people with a vested interest in the continuation of violence but the vast majority want to get on with the job of living in a peaceful society. To reach this desired goal it will be necessary for all to accept that Northern Ireland is a society of divided identities and that the contribution of each needs to be given its place. There is so much of Northern Ireland life which can be shared by all. There is the possibility of a healthy growth of a shared Northern Ireland identity.

3 The Saga of the Assembly. The rise and fall of power-sharing and after

When on 30 March, 1972, the Prime Minister, Edward Heath, prorogued the Northern Ireland Parliament it came as a shock to most people in Ulster. For Protestants at any rate this meant that at a stroke of the pen, their country had been deprived of its devolved measure of sovereignty—no-one under 60 years of age could really remember any other regime.

Apparently it also came as a shock for Northern Ireland's Prime Minister, Brian Faulkner, who had been summoned to Downing Street two days previously. In view of the unabating violence he anticipated a discussion on security methods and probably some new political initiative to involve the minority. Instead he was faced with the ultimatum that Westminster was to control all security, i.e. police as well as the army, or Heath would have to apply Article 75 of the Government of Ireland Act of 1920 and rule directly from Westminster. Faulkner discussed the matter with his cabinet and it was agreed that complete control of security was unacceptable to Stormont.

As soon as the measure was announced, hundreds of angry men from the shipyards marched through the centre of Belfast chanting 'Heath out—Enoch in'—Enoch Powell having been against this move. The following week William Craig addressed a large rally of his Unionist splinter group, the Vanguard Party, outside the Belfast City Hall. He called for a two day strike in protest to which it was estimated some 190,000 people responded. Some of these wanted to work and they complained of intimidation by Vanguard workers. On the second day there was a mass march of over 100,000 to Stormont, where they were welcomed from the balcony of Parliament Buildings by William Craig, who for the occasion had the support of an embittered Brian Faulkner appearing, to the surprise of many, at the right hand of Craig.

The British Government appointed William Whitelaw as Secretary of State for Northern Ireland together with three junior ministers, each of whom was given charge of various departments comprising Stormont's devolved responsibility. The policy in broad outline was (1) that there would be periodic plebiscites on the question of the border as a reassurance to the Protestant population that there would be no change in the British pledge to respect the wishes of the majority of the citizens of Northern Ireland; (2) a start would be made on phasing out internment and (3)

Westminster would accept full responsibility for law and order.

Naturally the response of the Catholic Social and Democratic Labour Party was reasonably positive. The 'Stormont' Parliament, which in effect meant the Unionist Party, blamed for so long for permitting anti-Catholic discrimination, was no more. The SDLP took a conciliatory line towards Protestants—'to our Protestant fellow citizens who differ from us politically we say this. We do not regard our political achievements as a victory over you. Rather do we see them as steps forward and as an opportunity for us all . . . we recognise that many of you feel isolated in the present circumstances. You are not. You are our fellow countrymen, and we are yours. Together a great opportunity awaits us. We ask you to join with us in meeting the challenge.' Westminster was asked to bring internment to a speedy end and to make sure that political arrests by the army and RUC would cease.

Brian Faulkner, at first bitter about the ending of his government, made a number of speeches to Unionist and Conservative Associations at home and in Great Britain, and during the summer to American audiences also, explaining his position. He realised he could never really make common cause with the Vanguard Party, threats of UDI and of strikes were not his method and he returned after an extended holiday to see his role as one of those trying to get the best possible conditions for some form of devolved government linked to Britain.

William Whitelaw and his ministers were to have plenty of trouble but not over administration. Northern Ireland had an efficient civil service whose principals were capable of independent thought. Wisely Westminster operated through this administration. Obviously the situation was ripe for misunderstanding and a clash of jealously guarded fields of operation between Whitehall and Stormont. From the viewpoint of the citizens of Northern Ireland any friction there was not noticeable. The big problem lay in administering a state rent by civil disorder and violence.

Certainly the violence was not ending, rather the bombing campaign was intensified. The Provisional IRA believed that it was their violence that had ended Stormont. If they kept up their campaign the British would find Northern Ireland too costly to govern and they would leave and go home.

William Whitelaw set about honouring his government's declared aims. By 23 April 1972 he had released 133 internees. By 8 June 520 had been released, leaving 416 still behind the Long Kesh wire. This number had dropped to 195 by the end of the year.

A Northern Ireland Border Poll Act was passed in 1972 enabling a referendum on attitudes to the border between Northern Ireland and the Republic. This poll was eventually held on 8 March 1973. In answer to the question 'Do you want Northern Ireland to remain part of the United Kingdom?' 591,820 or 57.5% of the electorate voted 'yes', while only

6,463 said 'yes' to the question 'Do you want Northern Ireland to be joined with the Republic outside the United Kingdom?' However, with 41% of the voters abstaining, one cannot tell how many would have voted 'yes' to the second question if the Catholic community had not been urged to boycott the poll. The exercise was thus of very little meaning.

Preparations for a new devolved government

William Whitelaw then sought ideas on the best type of government for Northern Ireland, not only from the known political parties, but from any organisation or individual. It was stated that he received about 2,500 submissions. Armed with this advice he invited the seven political parties of the Stormont House to send spokesmen to a conference to meet at Darlington on 25 September. Only three parties accepted, the Official Ulster Unionist Party, the liberal Alliance Party and the Northern Ireland Labour Party. The SDLP refused because Westminster still retained internment, Paisley's Democratic Unionist Party was at that period demanding complete integration with Britain and William Craig's Vanguard Party was still thinking in terms of a possible UDI.

There was no agreement, naturally, but William Whitelaw's 'Green Paper' was issued in 1972. It stressed that Northern Ireland must remain a part of the United Kingdom as long as the majority wished it, but that this did not preclude an 'Irish dimension'. This was the first time that this phrase had been used because, it is suggested, a member of the government service, taking notes at the Darlington Conference, coined the phrase as a shorthand for the recognition that the island of Ireland was shared with another government. The Westminster Government maintained it had to retain control of security as long as the army was involved. The Green Paper really prepared people for the White Paper published in March 1973, 'Northern Ireland constitutional proposals'[1] which were eventually embodied in the Northern Ireland Constitution Act 1973 (18 July). The main points were that Northern Ireland was to have a devolved assembly of 80 members, finally altered to 78, to be elected by proportional representation, single transferable vote system. The Secretary of State was to remain in office and to take the place of the Governor of Northern Ireland. This move was an unfortunate one as the Province had, in Lord and Lady Gray of Naunton, two representatives of the Crown who were dedicated to the task of serving the whole community. They had acted as non-political representatives of the Province as a whole, taking an active interest in events, actions and constructive endeavours in all sections of Northern Ireland life.

Westminster, as envisaged in the Green Paper, kept control of all security measures, but, it was hoped, would be able to hand over responsibility for the police, prisons, courts and criminal law in general as soon as the civil disturbances came to an end. Otherwise the devolved powers were very much as laid down for the Stormont regime by the Government of Ireland Act of 1920.

The election of this assembly took place on 28 June 1973, but before this Northern Ireland was to have, as it were, a rehearsal run on 30 May. This election was for the newly formed 26 District Councils (with much less power than the existing local Borough, Urban, Rural and County Councils) and was the first such election since 1967. For this reason probably there was a good poll, 68%, which is high for local government elections. It was also the first election since the twenties to be held on the basis of proportional representation. A number of candidates stood as independents, but there were over 200 Official Unionists and another 70 hard-line Unionists—'Loyalists'—returned for the 526 seats. The SDLP was the second strongest party with about 80 seats and the new Alliance Party, made up of Catholics and Protestants working together, polled 60 seats. The Northern Ireland Labour Party suffered badly and had only one member.

On the occasion of the Northern Ireland Assembly elections the Unionist Party was seriously split for the first time, though Brian Faulkner's Official Unionists did emerge as the largest single party with 23 seats out of the 78. When the splinter Loyalist groups were added this totalled 50 seats out of the 80. But these other Unionists were not pledged to follow Brian Faulkner's lead. The new Assembly divided thus:

Official Unionists		23
'Unpledged' Unionists	10	
Vanguard Unionist Progressive Party (William Craig leader)	7	
Democratic Unionist Party (Ian Paisley leader)	8	
West Belfast Loyalist Coalition	2	27
Social Democratic Labour Party		19
Alliance Party		8
Northern Ireland Party		1
		78

The Catholic opposition was represented by the SDLP. Some Catholics also voted for the Alliance Party, the latter being a liberal cross-bench group which along with the Northern Ireland Labour Party accepted the existing constitutional position.

This meant that Faulkner was able to call upon his 23 members, together with the SDLP, Alliance Party and NILP, another 28, to give 51 in all out of the 78 members in favour of power-sharing—a reasonable majority.

The Assembly met for the first time on 31 July 1973 but the next few months were taken up with periodic meetings to try to arrange which group was going to make policy. It was not until 22 November that William Whitelaw was able to go to the House of Commons and assemble a coalition cabinet of 11 members made up of 6 Unionists, 4 SDLP and 1 Alliance. There would also be another 5 non-voting members, 1 Unionist, 2 SDLP and 2 Alliance.

The Power-Sharing Executive

In the White Paper it had been stated that the leaders of the elected representatives to the Assembly would be invited, together with representatives of the Government of the Republic of Ireland, to talk with the Westminster representatives on how the aims of this White Paper might be realised.

Accordingly, on 5 December these groups were invited to the Civil Service Training College at Sunningdale in Berkshire. Only those three parties who agreed to make up the Executive attended from Northern Ireland. At the end of four days an agreed statement was issued. The guarantee was once again given by the British Government 'to support the wishes of the majority of the people of Northern Ireland'. Northern Ireland was part of the United Kingdom but 'if in the future the majority of the people of Northern Ireland should indicate a wish to become part of a united Ireland, the British Government would support that wish'.

It was recognised that the people of the Republic of Ireland, together with a minority in Northern Ireland, as represented by the SDLP, continued to uphold the aspiration of a united Ireland, but that the unity they wanted to see was a unity established by consent—'there could be no change in the status of Northern Ireland until a majority of the people of Northern Ireland desired a change in that status'.

Detailed plans were then laid down for the formation of a Council of Ireland with 30 members from the Republic and 30 members from the Northern Ireland Assembly. This revived the idea of such a council, which had been written into the original Government of Ireland (1920) Act but never implemented. The Northern Ireland Government was always resolutely against any such federal type institution which was seen as a means of severing the British link and ending the existing State of Northern Ireland.

The non-power-sharing 'unpledged' Unionists, led by Harry West, William Craig's Vanguard Unionist Progressive Party and Ian Paisley's Democratic Unionist Party, plus two West Belfast Loyalist Coalition members continued to be suspicious of the whole concept of having a cabinet where anti-partitionists had legislative power. Above all, they were against the idea of a Council of Ireland. It was in vain that Brian Faulkner explained that the Council was only consultative: it could only have the powers that the Assembly chose to give it. It could have given to the North, in Brian Faulkner's words, 'a formidable bargaining power which no Government in Dublin can ignore.'

As will be seen from the rest of this chapter, events overtook the new Executive before any plans for this Council could be worked out.

Power-sharing in action

In this first speech on 24 January Brian Faulkner outlined the Executive's plans for development in the Province. The economy had stood up remarkably well to riots, bombs, fires, hold-ups and bullets, and was at the time showing a faster rate of production growth than in the rest of the UK. What was needed was better training for the labour force to meet the needs of modern industry. A new Department of Manpower Services was being created to deal with this problem, while the Department of Housing, Local Government and Planning was concerned with re-activating the house building programme which had fallen badly behind, in the context of a planned scheme for the whole Province which included close co-operation with the 26 new District Councils.[2]

These and other issues were treated as a vote of confidence measure. The Executive had a majority of 51 to 27, which would allow for some defection from the supporting Unionist group, or from the SDLP.

The Executive, on assuming the reins of office, commenced work with commendable promptitude. They appeared to be working together, better than one had dared to hope. SDLP members were seen to be tackling the problems of their departments with enthusiasm and efficiency. John Hume, in charge of Commerce, was soon to leave for the USA to try to attract new industry to Ulster. Austin Currie, who had in the Stormont days squatted in protest against local council housing allocation policy, was put in charge of housing. Before long he was engaged in evicting Catholic squatters from rebuilt houses in an attempt to bring Protestants back into what had been a 'mixed street' in the Catholic Ardoyne area of Belfast. Paddy Devlin was making a success of his leadership of the Department of Health and Social Services and earning the respect of his civil servants. A Protestant legal member of the Executive, Basil McIvor at the Department of Education was tackling the difficult problem of integrated education and risking the opposition of the Catholic hierarchy by seeking a change in the law to facilitate the setting up of shared schools. He suggested discussions with the churches on this subject.

On 28 February an event took place which the new Executive could well have done without. This was the Westminster General Election, which resulted in the return of the Labour Party to power. In Northern Ireland, however, 11 of the 12 MPs returned were Unionists opposed to the power-sharing Executive. This event highlighted the fact that the concept of power-sharing did not have the support of the majority of rank-and-file Unionist voters. It could be claimed that the Executive Cabinet was undemocratic. Why, the argument ran, was Britain insisting on majority rule for Rhodesia when she was consistently denying it to Northern Ireland?

Brian Faulkner lost the party leadership of the Official Unionist Council, and in May 1974, he and his supporters in the Assembly broke from the main party and formed a new political group, the Unionist Party of Northern Ireland.

As well as spelling it out loud and clear that the Council of Ireland was only to be a consultative body, Faulkner, in his January speech, said that the Catholic community, representing one third of the population, had not played a commensurate part in the life and affairs of the Province. For this situation 'we can go on attributing mutual blame up to and beyond the point where the rest of the world grows sick of us. All I know is that we have now found the means to work together. Are we now, to say to that community "Democracy is simply majority rule and if that means you are to sit in opposition for half a century more it's just too bad"? I ask the opponents of all that we in this Executive represent "what is your answer?"'.[3] The answer lay in the deep irrational tribal fear well expressed in a bitter remark by a taxi driver: 'One of these days we'll wake up and find ourselves in the Free State' (i.e. the Republic of Ireland).

There was another factor which contributed to the fears of 'the Protestant in the street'. It seemed as if the SDLP controlled the Executive. In actual fact the Unionists at Sunningdale made sure that they controlled the vital departments—Finance, Education, Agriculture and the Environment—but where legislation touched the citizen's life it was found that the Minister in charge was a Catholic. You were vitally concerned about getting a house—Austin Currie was the spokesman. You were worried about your pension or supplementary benefit—Paddy Devlin answered the question. Bringing more jobs to the Province—John Hume was in charge. When it came to law reform the Alliance leader, Oliver Napier, was responsible, but he too was a Catholic. Then Gerry Fitt, as Deputy Minister, was on hand to make statements, so that it looked as if it was an SDLP Executive which had graciously agreed to share power with the Unionists and had put Faulkner up as a tame figurehead.

Trades Unions, the Ulster Workers' Council and their strike

Trades unions have always been bedevilled in Northern Ireland by sectarian loyalties, which in times of stress take precedent over union loyalties. Catholic workers owe allegiance not only to their church, but also to the concept of Irish Nationalism, which has a very strong emotive call. Protestant workers feel the strong emotive call to their Orange Lodge and to their church, though to a lesser degree than Catholics, but above all to the 'Protestant State'. Thus Protestant workers can parade one day as a result of normal trade union motives for better pay or working conditions, possibly alongside fellow Catholic union members, and then the next day, in a response to a tribal Protestant call, take part in a march against the desires of the fellow Catholic union members. The term Loyalist Association of Workers shows this allegiance. This organisation, LAW, drew its basic support from Harland & Wolff Shipyard workers. In 1971 they rented a room at the Unionist Headquarters in Glengall Street, Belfast, and went round factories all over the Province whipping up support.

By 1974 they had re-formed as the Ulster Workers' Council and claimed to represent some 300,000 Protestant workers. They had strong branches in the electricity power stations, particularly in the largest at Ballylumford at Larne.

On 14 May 1974 the Workers' Council issued an ultimatum stating that, if a motion was carried in the Stormont Assembly in support of the Sunningdale agreement, they would call a general stoppage. Brian Faulkner gained a 44 to 28 majority and four-hourly power cuts were imposed. Workers were called out from all factories and the UDA gave them support. The Vanguard Party gave the Workers' Council office space in their centre, a house in a very respectable area of Belfast and helped them with the organisation of the strike. On the first day of the strike the UK Minister, Stanley Orme, told the Workers' Council representative that they were bigots, and in general gave them short shrift. Subsequently the Secretary of State, in charge of security, steadfastly refused to negotiate with the strikers.

It appears that neither the British presence (the Northern Ireland Office) nor even the Executive quite appreciated what was happening. What started off as a protest by a small group of hard-line Protestant workers somehow seemed to touch a tribal emotive chord in the hearts of a considerable section of the Protestant population. Not all Protestants wanted the strike, but there were enough to man human barricades across many roads into and within Belfast. Unionist farmers also co-operated and there were stories of farmers who, though they lost milk because it could not be processed, and chicks because there was no power to keep incubators heated, nevertheless sat down and wrote cheques to support the Ulster Workers' Council saying, 'someone has to take a stand'.

The Irish Congress of Trades Unions also misread the strength of feeling. They were against the strike and accepted an offer from Len Murray, Secretary of the Trades Union Congress, to come to Ulster to speak to the Ulster Workers' Council. A march was planned to cross the

Lagan river bridge at Belfast Harbour to go to Harland & Wolff's Shipyards. Police protection was provided, but in the event only 200 people took part, and they met with considerable opposition from the crowd. It must have been the first time that the General Secretary of the TUC had ever led a strike-breaking march. In justice, it must be said that it was no normal strike; it was a sectarian or nationalist rally using, in the main, non-violent techniques.

So the strike progressed and the energy position worsened. A liberal ad hoc group (consisting mainly of members of reconciling bodies) went to see the Workers' Council. The aim was to dissuade them from completely wrecking the Ulster they desired to preserve. In particular the point was made that the breakdown of essential supplies would harm most of those least able to fend for themselves, children, the elderly, the handicapped. The Council replied that they could give an assurance that their welfare services would see that food supplies and alternative means of heating would be supplied to such groups. This they endeavoured to do over the next few days.

The Workers' Council admitted that they were supported by the UDA in various areas of the Province, but said that they had stressed there was to be no violence and that on no account were strikers to get into conflict with the army. Following an emotional meeting in Ballymena, a Protestant gang entered a public house and killed two Catholics. Some petrol stations were damaged and there were intimidating threats of violence against firms which did not close, and individuals who refused to strike. Although the strike therefore did not conform to the classic rules of non-violent activity, the whole exercise was conducted with a surprising absence of violence. The Provisional IRA called off their bombing campaign while they watched the Loyalists destroying their own state. Within a week, without the use of a single bomb, they saw the economy grind to a virtual halt.

Many people, including, naturally, the Catholic community, felt that the army should have been called in to man essential services. Merlyn Rees ordered more troops to Northern Ireland (there were about 16,500 at the time) but hesitated to use them—for one good reason—the army had had a look at the main power station and realised that they had not the expertise to man it. To attempt a take-over could have led to sabotage of the machinery and there was the risk of alienating a large section of the Protestant population which might have become a 'second front' to add to the problem of containing the violent Republicans.

For a few days one had the extraordinary situation of army blocks and searches on some roads, while UWC pickets attempted to close off others. The army did, however, keep the main roads open and the police claimed to have cleared 300 barricades throughout the Province, but as many were human barricades, they merely re-formed. In many areas the police were hopelessly outnumbered—there were at the time 4,300 for the

Province—and could not have taken any effective action. This was another vivid example, if one was required, showing that the police must have the support of the overwhelming majority of the population.

The RUC reported 862 road blockages, but there were only 71 people ever charged, most of them with disorderly behaviour and malicious damage—25 of these were in one town, Limavady.[4] The army did take some action during the period and on 26 May dawn raids were made on Protestant areas in Belfast, neighbouring Newtownabbey and Carrickfergus and 30 men were taken into custody, 18 still being held at the end of the day.

On the whole, road blocks consisted of peaceful pickets and if death or bomb threats were made they were not carried out. The writer found some workers rather embarrassed by their task and they would say, 'It is no use us letting you through; you will only be stopped further down the road'. If one indicated one's journey was of service to others, hospitals, welfare homes or other similar concerns, there was no impediment.

The UWC took control of most of those petrol stations they had allowed to remain open. Petrol was given out with the strikers' patronage. The moral issue then imposed itself. If one did not approve of the strike did one plead with the UWC for petrol dockets? There was some evidence that local authority and civil service staff, in dire need of petrol, did just this.

The fall of the Executive

On 27 May, the thirteenth day of the strike, Merlyn Rees decided to act, and he ordered army petrol lorries standing by to take over and supply 21 stations throughout Northern Ireland. The UWC called a press conference and stated that if the army was going to interfere then they could look after all the services such as milk, bread and animal feeding supplies: they would call for a complete shutdown.

Other serious problems arose. Sewage was not being pumped and in a low-lying area like Belfast the conditions were on the point of causing widespread sewage floods and contamination.

Brian Faulkner held meetings with his permanent secretaries and with the Executive and decided that to carry on would risk the lives of many. He therefore advised the Secretary of State to open talks with the Ulster Workers' Council. Merlyn Rees refused to do so and Faulkner and his Unionist colleagues in the Executive resigned. The others did not do so, but the next day, 29 May, Westminster prorogued the whole Assembly for four months. At the end of this period the Northern Ireland Act 1974 extended the period but on 28 March 1975 the Assembly was finally dissolved.

On 25 May at the height of the stoppages, Harold Wilson, as Prime

Minister, made a nationwide TV appearance. He called the strike organisers 'thugs and bullies', but the shaft that caused the bitterest wound was the comment that those who viciously defied Westminster after receiving £300 million per annum (the 1974 figure) in aid from Britain were 'spongers'. This helped to unite all types of Loyalists who felt it was a poor response to their continued loyalty—an underhand trick towards those who had lost several regiments in 1915 at the Battle of the Somme and who had suffered Nazi bombing during the Second World War, along with other British cities. Even Maire Drumm, the vice-president of Sinn Fein (later to be murdered in hospital) said, 'It makes me sick to hear an Englishman saying those things about Irishmen.'

So back came Direct Rule, with Gerry Fitt, the deputy leader of the Executive, describing the collapse as 'the saddest event in the political history of Northern Ireland'. Catholics, who had in the main been supporting the Executive, were angry and bitter, chiefly with the Northern Ireland Office for letting the UWC get away with the strike. Those Protestants in support of power-sharing were deflated and disheartened, but for the anti-Sunningdale power-sharing Protestants it was a time of triumph. It went some way towards restoring the national pride, which had received a rude shock when Stormont was prorogued two years previously. It was as if they could sing *mutatis mutandis*, with the Southern Nationalists, 'a nation once again'. They danced and sang in the streets of the Protestant ghettos as they do on the Twelfth of July, and they marched in triumph to the Stormont Parliament building, where they were joined, up the long stately panoramic drive, by Loyalist farmers driving their tractors, to pay tribute to the UWC and anti-Sunningdale leaders at the top of the steps.

Thus did Brian Faulkner relinquish leadership of the Province—for ever, as, sadly, three years later he met with a fatal riding accident. This one-time active Orangeman, who became an enthusiastic leader of a Joint Protestant-Catholic 'Cabinet' remains something of an enigma. He was not a Vicar of Bray, nor even just an ambitious career politician, and to understand the changes in his outlook during these later years of stress one cannot do better than read David Bleakley's biography of the leader.[5] Written in 1974, it was too soon to view Brian Faulkner's contribution in the context of the unrolling history of Northern Ireland, but it has the valuable freshness of contemporary evaluation. It is a sympathetic study by one who was a political opponent in the House, and who later, as a Northern Ireland Labour Party member, accepted an invitation from Brian Faulkner to serve in the Unionist Cabinet as Minister of Community Relations.

The Feakle meeting and a cease-fire

At the end of 1974 an event took place which should be mentioned, if only in parenthesis, as an example of church initiative.

From 9 to 11 December, in a clandestine atmosphere, an ad hoc group of churchmen met the leaders of the Provisional IRA in the little town of Feakle, in County Clare in the Republic. The church leaders, Protestant and Catholic, had made a joint call to peace in the North. They appeared together on TV and rallies were arranged for Belfast and other towns. They were able to persuade the Provisionals to call a cease-fire to last over Christmas. It was thought that the Provos might be persuaded to continue the cease-fire and this was communicated to the Secretary of State. The Northern Ireland Office negotiated with Provisional Sinn Fein and the cease-fire was first extended to 10 February and then extended indefinitely. The Northern Ireland Office agreed to look at any violence committed against the Provisionals who set up a number of 'incident centres' where such alleged breaches would be investigated.

The statistics in Appendix C show a considerable drop in the number of bombs placed and in shooting incidents. This did bring a feeling of relief in the Province; people began to move about with a greater sense of security and in particular, evening activities began to flourish again. But even so, by the end of the year, the number of civilian deaths had actually increased above the figure for 1974. The paramilitary Protestants' groups had carried out a number of retaliatory murders of Catholics and some of these were avenged. The number of happenings reported to the incident centres increased and dealt frequently with complaints about harassment by the army. The centre of activity moved towards the rural area of South Armagh. This hilly terrain provided, and has continued to provide, the guerrillas with good natural cover. It was near to the border, which could be easily crossed, providing sanctuary from the army and the RUC—though not from the Garda Siochena, the Republic's police force, who have made numerous arrests of IRA activists. During the cease-fire period it was thought that some of the action in South Armagh against Protestants living in the area and against the security forces was carried out by Republican splinter groups acting without reference to the Provisional IRA. At any rate the number of complaints dealt with at the incident centres increased, until their presence became farcical. They were closed down and the cease-fire ended. In 1976 there was an increase in sectarian tit-for-tat murders and the total killed was higher than in 1975, before dropping off appreciably in 1977 and the years following.

The right-wing element of most churches condemned the Feakle exercise. The Church, it was said, should not 'meddle in politics'—or 'give recognition to, or consort with, murderers'. A more reasonable assessment was to commend those who did not remain hidden in an ivory tower of pietism, but were willing to take the risks of becoming practical peacemakers.

The Constitutional Convention

Although prior to partition Unionists had not sought a devolved Parliament and preferred that government should continue from Westminster, after 50 years of a considerable amount of autonomy their views had altered. Apart from Paisley's Democratic Unionist Party (DUP), no-one at that time considered total integration with Britain to be a desirable alternative. Enoch Powell, representing the South Down constituency, was an exception, thereby embarrassing the Unionist Party leader, Harry West, whose party advocated the restoration of the Northern Ireland Stormont regime.

Westminster recognised the ending of the Assembly and the re-introduction of Direct Rule by the Northern Ireland Act 1974. This also provided for a Convention to consider 'what provision for the government of Northern Ireland is likely to command the most widespread acceptance throughout the community there'.

Under the name of the Secretary of State for Northern Ireland, Merlyn Rees's two discussion papers were produced. The first dealt with finance and the economy, the second the main parameters acceptable to the Westminster Government and within which the elected representatives should make their decision on the form of government acceptable. The terms were left very wide, including the extent of the devolved powers desired.

History had shown that in such a divided community no appreciable section of the community could, let alone should, be coerced into accepting the other's view. To achieve consensus 'there must be some form of power-sharing and partnership because no political system will survive or be supported unless there is widespread acceptance of it within the community'. Any agreement would also have to be acceptable to 'the people of the United Kingdom and to Parliament at Westminster'. Also, as Northern Ireland shared a common geographical border with the Republic of Ireland, this fact formed a special relationship, which must be recognised, i.e. 'there is an Irish dimension'.[6] The people of Northern Ireland had asked for an opportunity to discuss and seek agreement among themselves. Right, this was the opportunity.

Representatives both of the British Government and of the Republic of Ireland had been present at the Sunningdale Conference. This time at the Convention the representatives of the people of Northern Ireland would be on their own. If now majorities tried merely to coerce—to count heads and make no concessions towards the success of consensus—then the Convention would have 'failed the people of Northern Ireland'. 'The price of failure would be high.' 'There is no ready-made alternative solution.'[7]

Some voluntary reconciling organisations urged the candidates who were standing for the 78 Convention places to go there seeking a workable solution and not to remain tied to a pre-conceived and published party manifesto. Unfortunately the parties did put forward manifestos as though it were an election for a legislative assembly.

The elections which took place on 1 May 1975 returned 46 United Ulster Unionist Council members. This included the main Unionist Party, Paisley's DUP and Craig's Vanguard Unionist Party; 1 independent Loyalist; 17 Social Democratic Labour Party; 8 Alliance Party; 5 Unionist Party of Northern Ireland, Brian Faulkner's Party; 1 Northern Ireland Labour Party.

A Northern judge, Sir Robert Lowry, was appointed Chairman and the Convention got down to its business right away. It was soon apparent that there was to be little give or take. The UUUC took a strong stand against power-sharing with any Nationalist at Cabinet level. They made the point that there was no objection to Catholics per se, but that they would not work with a group whose aim was Irish unity and a break with the British link. They realised some concessions had to be made and so fell back on Brian Faulkner's 1971 suggestion, that advisory committees be formed to deal with industrial matters, environmental problems and the social services, some of which could be chaired by Catholics.

The SDLP, having tasted both Unionist rule and power-sharing, insisted on having a provision to guarantee their party some legislative say by right. They also refused to lay aside any thought of an Irish dimension. The Alliance Party suggested that the Chairmen of the Advisory Committees should automatically become members of the Cabinet. The Unionist Party of Northern Ireland, now a truncated remnant of the chief Unionist group in the Assembly, made suggestions that the Republic of Ireland should alter its constitution to renounce claims on the six Northern counties and that they should allow extradition of criminals for 'political crimes'. The way was left open for power-sharing once again.

The Northern Ireland Labour Party, represented by the lone figure of David Bleakley, also called upon the Republic to repeal the claim over the Northern counties contained in Articles 2 and 3 of the 1938 Constitution of Ireland. The SDLP were urged to abandon for 'the immediate future' their long-term aims towards a united Ireland. The Unionist majority existed and democratically this should be recognised. However, they recommended government by committees, these committees being composed of representatives of parties according to their numerical strength in the chamber. There was to be no enforced power-sharing at all. Committee Chairmen should make up the Cabinet. During the summer of 1975 there was a hint of compromise and a delegation drawn from the UUUC (led on this occasion by William Craig) met privately with the SDLP to seek some common ground. Then there appeared to be a change of view in the Unionist ranks and the talks were repudiated, William Craig's vote being the only one in favour of the continuation of the talks.

By 23 October the Unionists were asking the Convention to accept their draft as a majority finding. The SDLP refused, naturally, and the voting was 39 with 30 against. However, the Convention continued to meet for its stipulated six months and on 7 November it was agreed, 42 votes to 31, that the Unionist proposals coupled with the SDLP's reasons for rejecting them be sent to the Secretary of State.

An Alliance Party proposal to extend the Convention was heavily defeated and the Convention ended with the only consensus achieved being the fact that all parties wanted some form of devolved government.

All was not finally wound up, for it was announced that the salaries of the Convention members would be paid for another six months (as provided for in the 1974 Northern Ireland Act) and that they might be recalled. This did happen in February of 1976 but after four weeks of abortive discussion there was no break in the power-sharing deadlock and Merlyn Rees announced that Direct Rule would continue indefinitely.

Although the UUUC and SDLP did have another period of talks in the summer of 1976 which yielded nothing, it was clear that Westminster took the attitude that for the time being it had done everything reasonably possible to find some consensus and that they would have to get on with the job of making Direct Rule work and concentrate particularly on the problems of reducing the level of violence.

In September 1976 Merlyn Rees became Home Secretary and the former Defence Minister, Roy Mason, took over. Unionists welcomed the appointment but the SDLP criticised it, fearing that the new Secretary of State would take a stronger anti-IRA line which might lead to suffering in Catholic areas. In the event the level of violence dropped dramatically in 1977 (see Appendix C). Nevertheless sections of the Loyalist population thought that Roy Mason was not taking a strong enough line with the Provisionals. Led by Ian Paisley of the DUP and with the support of Ernest Baird, who had been in the Vanguard Party, another workers' strike was planned. The organisers hoped to repeat the position as in 1974 but this time Loyalist workers were not united and many went to work. There was not the same feeling abroad that the future of Northern Ireland was at stake. The technicians at the Ballylumford Electricity Station were again key men in the exercise and this time they decided not to strike.

More troops were called in but it was noticeable that they remained in the background and that it was the Royal Ulster Constabulary which took command. The RUC was active in removing road blocks and making arrests and after about ten days the strike collapsed. Roy Mason told Ulster workers they could stand 'ten feet tall'. It was good for the morale of the police and helped to re-establish their authority so badly shaken from the time when the army was used for riot control and the 'B' Specials were disbanded. It also showed the Catholic community that the police were willing to stand up to Protestant law breakers.

Roy Mason achieved a security triumph during the summer of 1977 when as part of the Silver Jubilee celebrations, the Queen, Prince Philip and the two young princes visited the Province in the royal yacht *Britannia*. The visit took place by chance at the time of the anniversary of the re-commencement of internment in 1977. There was a certain general apprehension lest the occasion should be used for a special show of violence. The SDLP, whose members would not have been anxious to emphasise the British link in any case, criticised the Northern Ireland Office for risking people's lives to satisfy the pride of the Secretary of State. Although a bomb was discovered near the site of one of the royal receptions the visit was carried out successfully and it helped to raise the morale—anyhow of the Protestant majority.

The defects of Direct Rule

There was in the province a wide hiatus between the 26 District Councils with limited remits and 'the government'—civil servants working under the guidance of the Secretary of State and his three Ministers. Who was to speak for the man in the street? His MP at Westminster was usually too remote and removed from the Northern Ireland scene. The field was wide open for any party or faction leader to claim he represented a large number of citizens. There was a need for some debating chamber to act as a sounding board for new ideas, or for complaints regarding government policy. Those taking part could be nominated by the Northern Ireland Office to represent a very wide spectrum of opinion and interest. A deputation in 1977 went from the 'Peace Forum' representing the majority of reconciling bodies in Northern Ireland to put this view to the Northern Ireland Office. It was explained to the deputation that the Northern Ireland Office had no plans for any such initiative at that time.

Ministers of State could not give all their time to their Northern Ireland departments. They had to be present at Westminster on occasions, for instance to answer parliamentary questions and to look after the interests of their own constituents. When under James Callaghan's Labour Government, Lord Peter Melchett was given charge of Education and Health and Social Services, he was freer to give more time to the task, being a member of the Upper House. He took an active interest in many educational, welfare and community projects as did his Conservative successors, Lord Elton and the Earl of Gowrie. All Ministers have made themselves available to receive delegations from all sorts of organisations—from groups making complaints, others lobbying for new legislation, or looking for grants-in-aid. A courteous and unhurried interview is usually given with the relevant civil servants present. It is a privilege to live in a small democracy where one may speak directly to the seat of power, but these visits are time-consuming for the machinery of government. They are also at times frustrating for the visiting participants, who usually feel that they have made a good case but find their plans have vanished into limbo. This is another reason for an open forum where complaints, aims and requirements may be tested against a body representing the whole Province.

There was a growing call for a new government initiative and in November 1977 Roy Mason did start seeing the leading political parties in yet another attempt to find an agreed basis for a devolved government. He stated that this was the Government's intention and if he could find any hopeful lead he said he would consider recalling the Convention. He tested out the possibility of what he termed 'interim devolution', which might in the first instance confer powers equal to a British local authority. The idea was received with little enthusiasm by the political parties, some feeling that such an interim policy might well become permanent. More devolved power was wanted.

In the Republic of Ireland, James Lynch, leader of the Fianna Fail Party, had won a resounding victory. He spoke as the new Taoiseach on Radio Telefis Eireann re-affirming his commitment to the eventual unification of Ireland. As a result, both the Democratic Unionist Party and Unionist Party withdrew from the talks as a mark of protest.

When the Conservatives won the election in May 1979, the new Secretary of State, Humphrey Atkins, took a period to review the situation. In the autumn of 1980 he proposed a conference to discuss the type of devolved government which might gain general acceptance. In November 1980 he produced a working paper on the proposed agenda; various solutions were ruled out at source, such as a return to the former Stormont regime, Irish unity or independence for Ulster.

Only the Alliance Party agreed unconditionally to participate, though the DUP gave a conditional acceptance. After some hesitation and bargaining on the part of the SDLP the Conference commenced on 7 January 1980, with rather curiously no representative from the mainline Unionist Party. A number of Unionists felt that their leader, James Molyneaux, had erred in this judgement as the field was wide open for Ian Paisley to represent the Unionist point of view. Towards the end of January 1980, however, the Unionist Party did make a written submission to the Conference. There was also one from a breakaway group, the Ulster Progressive Unionist Party and one from the Northern Ireland Civil Rights Association. Gradually an agenda was agreed though some groups refused to discuss certain items.

By the end of March 1980 14 items had been discussed, dealing with such topics as the type of powers to be transferred, whether the devolved body should have legislative as well as executive powers, whether there should be two houses or one and the whole problem of protecting the position of the minority, either by a Bill of Rights or some special method of appeal. There was no general consensus and the Secretary of State left to report the position to his Cabinet.

The summit meetings

On 8 December 1980 Margaret Thatcher went to Dublin for a summit meeting with the new Taoiseach, Charles Haughey, who had taken office when James Lynch retired. She took with her the Foreign Minister and the Chancellor of the Exchequer. The Ministers of External Affairs and Finance in the Republic were also present. They were to examine 'possible new institutions, structures, citizenship rights, security matters, economic co-operation and measures to encourage mutual understanding'. It was obviously quite a high-powered meeting and it caused an uproar in Northern Ireland. Margaret Thatcher insisted that nothing said in Dublin would prejudice the Union. Any structure set up would be 'institutional' and not 'constitutional' and she repeated her assurances on the future of Northern Ireland within the United Kingdom. Ian Paisley was not assured and was convinced that arrangements would be planned to barter Northern Ireland for some British advantage. His suspicions were not allayed when the Republic's Premier spoke of the Dublin meeting as a step towards solving problems in Northern Ireland and especially when in March 1981 his Minister for External Affairs said in an interview that the meetings could lead to unity in ten years, remarks which Humphrey Atkins claimed were misleading. It would have been wiser if Margaret Thatcher had taken one of the eleven Northern Ireland MPs at Westminster with her to Dublin. He could have been present as an adviser on Northern Ireland matters: he would have represented 'the Northern Ireland dimension' at the talks.

Ian Paisley meanwhile gathered 500 men for the benefit of the press 'on an Antrim hillside'. Each man waved a slip of paper, said to be an official licence for his gun. This was but a sample of the numbers of men with guns that could be rapidly produced, it was explained, if Margaret Thatcher tried to end Britain's link with Northern Ireland. Then followed a series of rallies and open-air meetings led by Ian Paisley to pledge support for the maintenance of this British link and for the cause of Loyalist Ulster—on what was called, in remembrance of the anti-Home Rule Bill days, 'the Carson trail'. Margaret Thatcher paid two visits to Ulster principally to restore confidence among Protestants.

Having reviewed the findings of his 1980 discussions, on 2 July 1981 Humphrey Atkins announced a new initiative for Northern Ireland. In a speech in the House of Commons he said, 'There is not enough of a Northern Ireland political input into the government of the Province.'

Fully devolved government with legislative power was not possible at that time and it was necessary to have 'a more gradual approach.' Accordingly the Government had decided to form a nominated Northern Ireland Council of 50 members made up of Ulster Westminster MPs, European Parliament MPs and District Councillors. An elected body would have been preferable but to arrange such an election would take too long. Nominations were to be sought from the three groups concerned by the political parties roughly on their electoral strengths and submitted to the Northern Ireland Office for approval. Their role would be advisory only, but they would be asked to advise on a future governing body with executive and legislative powers.

All the leading parties in turn rejected the proposal, for differing reasons. The DUP would not partake as long as Margaret Thatcher continued secret meetings with the leaders in the Republic; the SDLP because there was no 'Irish dimension', but in general the political opinion was that the time had come for something more positive. Thus a measure which might have filled the gap between the District Councils and Westminster, some years previously, now proved to be a non-starter.

In September Margaret Thatcher withdrew Humphrey Atkins in a Cabinet re-shuffle, and replaced him by James Prior. It was rumoured that James Prior was going to refuse to leave the Ministry of Employment, where he was happy, but in the end he arrived and results were expected from a man of action. However, instead of being given a period of relative calm to take stock of the situation after the hunger strike, he was soon to be plunged into another emotional upheaval.

The Joint Working Party set up at the December 1980 summit reported on 2 November 1981. The report contained nothing about the constitutional position of Northern Ireland, but dealt with the rights and privileges accorded to citizens of each country, and in particular those rights available where citizens of one country were residing in the other state. The fields covered were the voting laws, social security, employment and consular protection. Some anomalies were noted; for instance whereas the 500,000-odd Irish citizens living in Great Britain can vote in British elections, only resident Irish citizens may vote in Irish general elections. The Taoiseach told the Prime Minister in December 1980 that he was prepared to put forward proposals to alter this situation.

Another summit meeting was held in November, this time in London, and with Garret Fitzgerald as the new Taoiseach. His Fine Gael party had ousted the Fianna Fail party of Charles Haughey only because Fitzgerald was able to form a coalition with the Irish Labour Party to give him a slender majority in the Dail.

Frequent assurances would not satisfy Ian Paisley that some secret deal involving the constitutional position of Northern Ireland had not in fact been arranged, and he called Margaret Thatcher a 'liar and a traitor'.

When he refused to withdraw the remark he was suspended from the House, but while the House of Commons Committee was deciding what final penalty should be imposed, the Unionist MP for South Belfast, Robert Bradford, was shot on 14 November. The warden of the Youth Centre in which Robert Bradford was carrying out his constituency business was also shot when he tried to prevent the assassins. This made eleven deaths in ten days, and Protestant patience was at breaking point. Both the DUP and the Official Unionists blamed the Northern Ireland Office for not providing sufficient security. James Molyneaux, for the Official Unionists, said that they would set up an information service to aid the army and police, and Ian Paisley for the DUP threatened to bring into action what was termed a 'third force' to take more positive action against the IRA. It might involve the use of weapons, he stated, if the army and police did not show greater urgency and efficiency. Parades of such groups took place in several towns, notably in Newtownards.

On the Monday following the Saturday shooting of the MP a large crowd, possibly 15,000, gathered for a memorial service at the City Hall War Memorial. There were disgraceful scenes a few days later in and around the church where Robert Bradford's funeral service was held. An appeal for a devout attitude had to be made before the service could proceed. James Prior attended the funeral and his bodyguard was hard put to enable him to gain access to the church without being manhandled.

The polarising effect of the emotion-charged scene following the deaths of the ten hunger strikers is looked at in the next chapter. The death of the first two hunger strikers made it very difficult for candidates of the Alliance Party and the Northern Ireland Labour Party at the local council elections held in May 1981. Only one NILP candidate was elected. During 1981 the remains of Brian Faulkner's Unionist Party of Northern Ireland, led by Anne Dickson, finally ceased to function as a party. The Social Democratic Labour Party found itself under considerable pressure not to lose voters to the Republican groups supporting the hunger strikers. They had already lost chief 'Labour' support when Gerry Fitt, and later Paddy Devlin, resigned, basically because they felt that the party was leaning too far towards its nationalistic green Irish dimension to the detriment of the needs of the Catholic worker.

The death of Robert Bradford MP brought to a head the already existing struggle for power between the Official Unionists and Ian Paisley. It is highly unlikely that immediately following the deaths of the hunger strikers and the shooting of the MP, the figures given in the opinion polls in Appendix B would apply. The moderate centre groups would be the sufferers, and the DUP would most likely show an increased following. Inflamed tribal and national emotions do not remain at boiling point for ever. As the temperature lowers, other factors, the employment situation and the cost of living, re-assume a more vital role in the minds of voters.

This is not to say that the task of restoring 'a Northern Ireland political input into the government of the Province' is going to be easy for James Prior or anyone else, but there is in 1982 a feeling that something must again be attempted.

4 Violence, justice and the law
The army as peacekeepers

In 1969 it became clear that the 3,052-strong police force in Northern Ireland was unable to cope with the large scale riots in Londonderry and Belfast. The Inspector General of the RUC made a request to the GOC Northern Ireland for the help of troops, first of all in Londonderry and a few days later in Belfast.

There were 300 men on hand at a Londonderry naval base, but apart from them only a token force was available from the four Northern Ireland army barracks and 608 troops had to be flown in hurriedly. They were moved to the Falls ghetto area in Belfast, where after a few days of rioting five Catholics and two Protestants had been killed and 270 homes completely burnt out (as well as a similar number damaged), the great majority of these being occupied by Catholic families.

Although ostensibly the troops came to keep both rioting sides apart, in fact this meant protecting Catholic homes from being invaded and harassed by Protestant mobs. Troops were welcomed by Catholics as protectors and mistrusted by Protestants who lived in the neighbouring ghetto area. There is evidence that some members of the army regiments who came for a four months' period of duty at this time thought they would be liable to be sniped at by Protestants. Certainly, traditional Protestant respect for the army vanished rapidly when it was found that they did not dismantle the barricades across some Catholic streets.

Power was given to the Commanding Officer, General Freeland, to order the disarming of any armed organisations in any area the army was patrolling. In Belfast and Londonderry the 'B' Special Police were asked to hand in their rifles pending an enquiry into the structure of the Royal Ulster Constabulary. A committee under the chairmanship of Lord Hunt set to work on 26 August 1969 and reported to the Ministry of Home Affairs on 3 October. The main recommendations were that the RUC 'should be relieved of all duties of a military nature as soon as possible', and that the carrying of arms by the police should be phased out. Credit was paid to the devotion to duty on the part of the Ulster Special Constabulary, known as the 'B' Specials, but they were to be disbanded and invited to join 'a locally recruited part-time force under the control of the army'. This was to become the Ulster Defence Regiment. The Northern Ireland police were to be organised very much as were the police in Great Britain and were not to be armed. It was not long before events showed, however, that Northern Ireland was not Great Britain and the trend was reversed but, at the time, the Report was accepted and the RUC patrolled for the first time unarmed and the 8,481 Special Police were disbanded.

The Protestant hard core felt that this 100% Protestant reserve force, their chief means of protection, had been taken away and a pro-Catholic army substituted.

The temper of Protestant workers was rising, especially in the area adjoining the Catholic Falls ghetto area of Belfast. There had been odd scuffles with the army and on Saturday night following the publication of the Hunt Report, crowds began to gather on the Shankill. The RUC and 'B' Specials formed barriers to stop the crowd advancing on the newly-built, Catholic-occupied 'Unity Flats' at the City end of the Shankill Road. The crowd tried to break through the cordon. Some of them had guns and a RUC constable was shot and killed. The army moved in to assist, using CS gas to disperse the crowd. After the gas had broken up the crowd the mob regrouped and shots were fired by snipers. The army eventually returned fire and two Protestants were killed.

In the light of future events this aspect of the struggle is often forgotten. In general, the population was thankful to have the army on the streets as an insurance against a repetition of the August riots. The intensity of Protestant reaction at that time had really frightened Catholic city dwellers and many Protestants in the Province were shaken and ashamed of what had, in effect, been done in their name.

Already General Freeland had warned that the honeymoon period of army acceptance was liable to be of short duration. His prophecy was to prove distressingly correct but, during the autumn and winter of 1969/70, the army did take the heat out of the situation and act as a genuine 'peace-keeping' force. It was as a short-term, anti-riot group that its role was envisaged, to be phased out as soon as the temperature had cooled enough to allow the reorganised police force to take over, backed by the mainly part-time Ulster Defence Regiment, which was set up in January 1970. This latter was envisaged as a non-sectarian peace-keeping force under the army, but one which as well as including former 'B' Specials also included 18% of Catholics in the initial recruitment period.

Problems of policing a divided society

This was the time to phase out the army, but there were three factors which made this appear impossible. Firstly, the RUC was not acceptable in Catholic areas. Tolerated by Catholics prior to 1968/69, events in Londonderry (when the RUC broke up the 5 October Civil Rights march with baton charges and in January 1969 when it entered the Bogside, taking the law into its own hands) convinced Catholics in the ghetto areas that it was a sectarian force not to be trusted. The second feature was the other side of the same coin—the police had suffered a shattering blow to their morale which was only to be regained slowly over the years. The very fact that the army was required on the streets meant that for the first time for over 50 years, the police had failed (with the help of the 'B' Specials) to restore law and order. Although it was acknowledged that the relatively small numbers of police had been very severely stretched, their handling of the events in Londonderry in 1968 had been condemned by the Cameron Commission reporting on these early demonstrations.[1] In 1972, the report of the Commission looking into the August 1969 disturbances (the Scarman Report) in a general commendation of the RUC, did find that on six occasions, the police were seriously at fault.[2] It was not surprising therefore that relations between the army and the RUC were at times strained.

In a society where tribal sectarian divisions make the achievement of political consensus very difficult to obtain, the police are also in a difficult position. Parliament makes the laws of the land as the result of a majority vote. The police must uphold the law. Thus, if you are a member of the minority which regards the law makers as biased against you, then you tend to be up against the police, whose job it is to enforce these laws. Events in Northern Ireland have shown all too poignantly that if the police are going to keep the peace in the classical manner, i.e. to find, arrest with the minimum of force and bring before the courts the law breaker, then the police must have the vast majority of the population behind them. What then happens if considerable sections of the population are not behind the police? This is a situation which does not occur in Great Britain. Some elements of such a situation were present in the 1926 General Strike, but a closer parallel to the Northern Ireland situation is to be found in the recent racial problems affecting areas of British cities. It is just not possible to arrest, try and incarcerate thousands of citizens. As long as a sizeable minority remains non-violent there is in civil disobedience a very strong method of bringing the attention of the majority to face the claims of injustice. When the minority becomes violent, its members invite violence against themselves and they forfeit the sympathy their cause might rightly claim. The obvious answer is to meet with and listen carefully to the claims of the minority. However, in Northern Ireland the situation is, as usual, complicated by the fact that there is a faction loud in its proclamation against the rightness of the claims of the minority, threatening to take the law into its own hands and use armed force if these claims are acceded to. If the faction is comparable in numbers to the size of the police force, how can the police enforce any unacceptable law without becoming an 'army' itself? In the Northern Ireland context, a Loyalist armed group might outnumber the police several times over.

Even when there is general consensus regarding the laws of the land, the police require more than passive support from the citizens. There must be a willingness to cry 'stop thief' and possibly risk physical injury through involvement. Otherwise old women will be mugged in greater numbers because people fear being involved.

Where, however, there are armed guerrillas operating, the situation alters in kind rather than degree. It is not reasonable to ask a member of the public to risk death at the hands of men who would not hesitate to take life in the cause of what is mistakenly thought to lead to national fulfilment.

This emergence of the guerrilla is the third reason why is has proved difficult to get the army back to barracks and off the streets. It began with an event early in 1970 which passed almost unnoticed by the majority in Northern Ireland. It was to have profound effects.

The advent of the armed guerrilla

There was a split at the Sinn Fein Annual Conference in Dublin. The main body of the movement took a Marxist stand, following the failure of its 1956–62 campaign against 'British' border installations. The IRA had abandoned violence as a tactic and were working towards a People's Republic for the whole of the 32 counties in Ireland; this would involve winning over at least a section of Protestant workers. As long as the Republican movement was geared into this line it was an assurance of peace; you don't unite with Protestant workers by shooting their policemen or scaring them with tales of warlike Gaelic heroes. Some Republicans, however, were impatient with this approach. They had been stung into action by the criticism and jeers of fellow Catholics in the North—especially in Belfast—who asked where were the much vaunted IRA when the Protestant mobs raided the Falls. The graffiti, 'IRA—I ran away' was hard to take and so they formed a separate military wing of Sinn Fein—a Provisional Army, first of all to protect Catholic areas. The name 'Provisional' had a strong Republican historical significance as in the 1916 uprising in Dublin Sinn Fein had proclaimed itself to be the 'Provisional Government of the Irish Republic'. In 1970 the first thing the Provisionals had to do was to build up their armed strength which was then virtually nil. It was made easier for them to store arms in their homes in the early months of 1972 as the army was respecting a number of Catholic housing estates as 'no-go areas', where the inhabitants were left to do as they pleased.

Fate played further into the 'Provos'' hands when the army began to become unpopular in certain Catholic areas. An early example of how this came about was seen at Ballymurphy, a West Belfast Catholic housing estate. It was the first estate built in the post-1945 building plan and had been used by the housing section of Belfast Corporation for placing problem families, often with a bad work record. There was always a high level of unemployment there, but it had not been affected by the rioting in 1969, in spite of having a Protestant estate right beside it. However, in April 1970, a Scottish regiment was stationed almost on the estate and the rumour went round that the regiment contained men from Glasgow who were strongly anti-Catholic. Youths stoned the troops, who replied by making 'snatch' raids into the area and arresting ringleaders.

It became clear that arms were being stored on both sides. A number of Protestants held guns, for which they had licences, some belonged to voluntary Rifle Clubs and there were rumours that some of the 'B' Special Police reserves had secretly retained their guns. In July 1970 General Freeland made an intensive search in the Lower Falls area for weapons. Reginald Maudling had paid his first visit to Belfast, as the Home Secretary, in place of James Callaghan, following the Conservative victory in the General Election. The GOC had been under pressure from the Northern Ireland Premier to go into the Catholic areas, and it is generally assumed that the Conservative Government encouraged this. The army cordoned off the whole area and imposed a curfew. Opposition was met by the use of CS gas—effective no doubt in dispersing a mob in the open air but quite unacceptable in the narrow confined streets of the Lower Falls, where the elderly and those with respiratory trouble suffered acute discomfort.

During the 34 hours of curfew five civilians were killed, 15 soldiers and 60 civilians injured. Some pistols, rifles and automatic weapons were found but the net result was to alienate whole Catholic areas against the army.

This search was the real beginning of the end of phase one of the army in Ulster, which consisted of riot control and protection of Catholic areas. Catholics still wanted the army around in case of a Protestant armed invasion, but they did not want troops coming into their housing estates. This Lower Falls exercise gained some support for the Provisional IRA who tried to pass themselves off as protectors of these Catholic areas. What was to prove more vital and dangerous was that the Provisional IRA began to make an appeal to Catholic youth in a way that the IRA in its 1956–62's 'Border' Campaign never achieved.

As the army persisted with search operations, relations with Catholics continued to deteriorate. The first killing of a soldier on the streets happened in February 1971, and on 10 March three young off-duty Scottish soldiers were lured out of a bar, taken up a country lane outside Belfast and shot through the head. Although this cold-blooded murder was not claimed by the Provisional IRA, the population on all sides was shocked and it did harm to the Provos' image.

The re-introduction of internment

All this was eclipsed by an event in August of that year (1971). The Prime Minister, Chichester-Clark, who was finding it increasingly difficult to hold his Unionist colleagues together, resigned in favour of Brian Faulkner. Brian Faulkner's answer to the increasing violence and the well nigh impossible task of obtaining evidence with which to convict the men of violence, was to re-impose internment without trial under the Special Powers Act. The decision was his alone, not that of the army or Westminster, and his Cabinet was not even recalled from the summer recess. Internment had been resorted to during the second world war (as in Britain under regulation 18B) and again during the IRA campaign 1956–62. Many in Ulster who found the expediency distasteful, expected that taking 300 men of violence out of circulation on 9 August would at least give some respite and a chance to stabilise the country and allow the new reforms to operate.

Presumably this was the thinking of the leading Protestant churches in Ireland whose spokesmen commended the operation. It was not long, however, before it became apparent that this assumption was far from correct. Some of those lifted were soon released and had quite obviously not been involved in violence. Others who had been members of the old IRA had been living as peaceful citizens for years. On one or two occasions the army, on whose shoulders the task of apprehending mainly rested, lifted the wrong man. Some of the leaders, having got wind that something was afoot, vanished, probably to the Republic. Even worse followed. Allegations were made of torture during arrest and interrogation. Even allowing for some exaggeration, the situation savoured too highly of Gestapo methods. A Group of Three was appointed by the British Government under the Chairmanship of the UK Ambassador, Sir Edmund Compton, to look into these allegations.[3] They reported in November of that year that of the 20 individual allegations made to them, none was classed as being physically brutal, though some constituted physical ill-treatment. Methods used consisted of such practices as keeping the suspects standing with their hands in front of them up against a wall for long periods, of being hooded, and being subjected to continual noise, deprivation of sleep and a diet of bread and water.

The question then arose as to what methods of interrogation could be used and three Privy Councillors under Lord Parker were appointed to examine the issue. This Committee was not able to agree on the condemnation of these practices, although Lord Gardiner, in a minority report, did condemn the practices unequivocally and the Government adopted his findings.[4]

The Government of the Republic of Ireland selected 14 of the 20 cases to bring before the European Court of Human Rights. After a long delay (in

January 1978), the Court found very much as the Compton Commission had done, namely that these practices did not amount to torture, but stated they were 'undoubtedly inhuman and degrading'.

This whole distressing practice came into the category of 'It can't happen here', and when it did, the reaction of decent people was not sufficiently condemnatory. Many Catholics thought that the Compton wording was dishonest. Protestants took comfort in the fact that the practices were officially condemned and put it out of their minds. Compensation was, in fact, paid to 12 of the men in whose names charges were preferred. The amounts involved were about £10,000 per case—though little publicity was given to these payments. Britain was able to state that the practices had been discontinued. Even so, they were to rear their ugly heads again and the next occasion involved Loyalists as well. In 1971 all the early internees were taken only from the Catholic community and in protest most Catholics in honorary public offices withdrew their services. Those Catholics living in statutory housing withheld their rents and some house owners refused to pay rates.

Internment, instead of bringing peace, led to rioting on a much greater scale than hitherto. Deaths due to civil disturbances increased from 25 in 1970 to 174 in 1971. Nearly all of them occurred after the re-introduction of internment. A bombing campaign in the cities of Belfast and Londonderry increased the number of explosions from 170 in 1970 to 1,515 in 1971 (see Appendix C).

Early in January 1972, a tragic event occurred which was to have wide and harmful repercussions. An anti-internment march had been planned by the Northern Ireland Civil Rights Association for 30 January in Londonderry.

Marches had been declared illegal since 4 August 1971 but the Association nevertheless decided to go ahead. On the advice of the head of the police in Londonderry, it was agreed not to enforce the ban as this would have caused even more violence. It was thus decided to allow the march to take place in the Catholic Creggan and Bogside Estates but to contain it in these areas by army control.

There had already been some sniping at soldiers in this area and it was considered highly probable that gunmen might take advantage of the confrontation between the crowds, police and army to open fire on the army. Troops are permitted to fire on their own initiative only when requiring to save their own lives or the lives of others. Where possible a soldier must give a warning. The Londonderry march reached the army's barricade. Soldiers who claimed they had identified gunmen opened fire in self-defence. Something went terribly wrong and the firing appeared to be indiscriminate. A number of marchers were hit and 13 were killed.

There was a wild outcry and a day of mourning proclaimed by the Catholic community in the North. Reaction in Dublin led to a mob burning down the British Embassy. There is, of course, deep cause for concern when peacekeepers take life, but political capital was made out of this tragic event.

Some attempt had to be made to investigate what looked like quite irresponsible action on the part of the army and the unenviable task fell to a High Court Judge, the Rt. Hon. Lord Widgery.[5] A large number of witnesses, civilian and military, were heard. The soldiers swore under oath that the people against whom they had fired were, in their opinion, about to use a weapon to endanger life. However, it was established that none of those killed had firearms of any sort on their persons. Nevertheless, the judge was satisfied that there had been shooting earlier from the area concerned and that some people in the march had firearms on them. From the evidence, it appeared that some of the soldiers had forgotten about the strict rule regarding the use of firearms only in self-defence, but the nearest Lord Widgery would go to apportioning blame was to say, 'At one end of the scale some soldiers showed a high degree of responsibility; at the other, notably in Glenfada Park, firing bordered on the reckless. These distinctions reflect differences in the character and temperament of the soldiers concerned.' Finally, the Tribunal remarked that no training could ensure that a soldier will always act wisely and that an individual soldier ought not to have to take this decision in a confused situation as on 30 January. In Northern Ireland, he noted, it was often inescapable.

Catholics, especially in Londonderry, regarded this as just a piece of biased whitewash. Lord Widgery appeared to be adding insult to injury when, in his opening statement of the conclusion, he made a seeming platitude that there would have been no deaths 'if those who organised the illegal march had not thereby created a highly dangerous situation in which a clash between demonstrators and the security forces was almost inevitable.' Protestants, also shocked at the event, would not have felt this statement to be a platitude and thought rather, 'What can the army do when people defy the law and make trouble for the army who have enough to cope with without this?' Only a very extreme minority of their number would have supported the callous gloating behind a piece of graffiti seen in Belfast, 'Paras 13—Provos 0'. It did not escape the notice of the Catholic community that no member of the security forces appeared to have been in any way reprimanded for the internment brutalities or the Londonderry shootings. Damages were later awarded, out of court, to the relatives of those shot, but nothing could undo this sad event which served to underline the fact that an army, especially a paratroop regiment, untrained in crowd or riot situations, was quite unsuited to deal with a situation such as this.

The problems of a UN peacekeeping force

From time to time, the query is raised regarding the feasibility of replacing the army by an international United Nations peacekeeping force. At the height of the August 1969 rioting, Dr. Hillery, then the Minister of Foreign Affairs for the Republic of Ireland, suggested that the police should be replaced either by an Anglo-Irish force or by a UN international one. When the idea was turned down at Westminster, Dr. Hillery persisted by raising the matter at the UN in New York. He was unable to have the issue raised in the Security Council for, as Lord Caradon correctly pointed out for Britain, under Article 2 Subsection 7 of the UN Charter, the UN is not authorised to intervene in matters which fall essentially within the domestic jurisdiction of any state.

Although this rule would not prevent Great Britain from requesting the UN for policing aid, it would be an unprecedented step by a sovereign state—a state which is also one of the original and permanent members of the Security Council. It is not a foregone conclusion that other states, particularly the Warsaw Pact countries, would welcome this opportunity of scoring over Britain. Too much enthusiasm on their part could lead to pressure being applied to them to accept UN troops should they find themselves confronted on some occasion by an irredentist rising in their own territory.

The general thought in Northern Ireland is that the British army finds it difficult enough where there is no racial differentiation, and no uniforms are worn, to know who is a paramilitary operator and who is, for example, a peaceful, non-political leader of a local youth club. The complexities of a situation where the gunman can fade into the local population would make the task almost impossible. The suggestion is made that even if members of a UN peacekeeping force could speak English, the local accent would prove incomprehensible!

An international force operates best where opposing factions are divided geographically and where some security can be given by assuring one or both sides of protection from attack. If some workable agreement for Northern Ireland's constitution and form of government could be arrived at, then a UN Observer Corps might be invited to serve as an unbiased monitoring group to see that the terms of the agreement were kept.

Direct Rule from Westminster

Edward Heath's government at Westminster had been watching with growing concern the increasing violence in Northern Ireland. Bloody Sunday was followed by a reprisal IRA bomb at the Parachute Regiment's HQ at Aldershot, an event which possibly focused the attention of Westminster on the fact that Brian Faulkner's government was not making progress. Westminster decided that a new initiative was required.

An ultimatum was put to Brian Faulkner on 22 March 1972 stating that the United Kingdom Government had decided to take over control of all branches of security including the police, the courts and the prisons. Faulkner refused as this would leave him in the position of a colonial administrator for Westminster. Edward Heath at once applied the final supreme power given under Section 75 of the Government of Ireland Act and prorogued the Northern Ireland Government.

As the first Secretary of State under direct rule, William Whitelaw found himself with a small province to administer and one where law and order were rapidly disintegrating. There were some 500 men interned without trial and an unknown but growing section of the Catholic population appeared willing to take up arms against the state or to support those who did. As was seen in Chapter 2, a section of the Protestant majority was angered at the ending of Stormont. They watched their cities, particularly Londonderry and Belfast, being increasingly molested by bomb attacks while the perpetrators either vanished into the Catholic 'no-go' areas or across the border into the Republic of Ireland, to join with their colleagues who were engaged in military type training. The Ulster Defence Association (UDA) then set up their own no-go areas behind barricades and their own quasi-military units paraded a uniform of khaki safari jackets and forage caps, with dark glasses and handkerchiefs over their faces to avoid detection. They made it quite clear in press, radio and television interviews that they were ready to fight in defence of Ulster if the Government fell down on the job.

In early July the Provisionals announced a cease-fire, possibly to see what would be the outcome of a secret meeting with the Secretary of State in London. Presumably they were not satisfied, for they seized upon an insignificant incident in a West Belfast housing estate to break the truce 13 days later. They leaked the fact of the interview later, which served to increase the suspicions of the UDA that the British Government was not to be trusted.

The Province was badly shocked on 21 July when 22 bombs went off virtually concurrently in Belfast on what became known as 'Bloody Friday'. Nine people were killed and 130 injured.

At the end of the month the army took down the remaining barricades and entered all areas in an operation known by the code word 'Motorman'. Trouble was feared, especially in the largest of the 'no-go' areas, Londonderry. In the event it all passed off peaceably enough, but in answer three car bombs went off unannounced in the little village of Claudy, 12 miles from Londonderry, killing seven people.

The Provisionals always make the point that they do not wish to kill Irish people, unless they disregard the warning given and go and work for the 'British', i.e. serve in the army, police, Ulster Defence Regiment or as a member of the prison staff. Warnings of active bombs having been planted in Northern Ireland (this would not apply to enemy territory 'Great Britain') are nearly always given. On 'Bloody Friday' the Provisionals claim that the police failed to act with sufficient promptitude and that they were not responsible for the Claudy bombs.

The UDA agreed after 'Motorman' to take down any barricades they had erected and the army assisted in this operation. The 'Loyalists'' answer to IRA violence was a campaign of assassination. It was not always clear whether those responsible were acting for the UDA, the Ulster Volunteer Force (UVF) or some other splinter group such as the Ulster Freedom Fighters, or even just a few acting on their own following a drinking session in a club. The victims as often as not had nothing to do with violence. This was curious as these extreme Loyalist groups had claimed that if the UDA and 'B' Specials had been left in control they could have dealt with the IRA as they knew who the IRA were and would have 'gone in and flushed them out'. These Loyalist assassinations were answered by some tit-for-tat shooting by Republican groups, but as the army seemed to be gaining the upper hand these assassinations were called off by the UDA and virtually ceased by 1977.

In 1972 an increasing number of Protestants were being arrested for having and, at times, for using, weapons, or for having bomb-making materials. A gable end on the Shankill Road bore the words 'Jails full of Prods', the inference being that this was a treacherous action. The RUC, they felt, would be better employed in finding and arresting Provos instead of those who in the final analysis were helping the police and the army to bring to an end the Republican violence. Catholics on the other hand were aggrieved that Protestants were charged and got off with seemingly light sentences for offences which on the Catholic side led to indefinite periods of internment in the Long Kesh internment centre.

The chief reason for this situation was that the police did not operate in the Catholic areas. Here the army made the arrests and they were not trained in gathering evidence which would lead to a conviction. The police operating in Protestant areas obtained convictions, the army relied on internment.

Evidence has been produced to show that at this time Catholic sentences were on average more severe than Protestant sentences for similar crimes.[6] Jury service was based on ownership of property and this tended to mean that, for example, in Belfast there were more Protestant jurors than the expected proportion. The prosecution was allowed to challenge any number of jurors, while the defence was only allowed to challenge up to 12 jurors per defendant without giving any reasons, though for a good reason they might exclude a larger number. Protestant defendants challenged Catholic jurors on the grounds that they might be biased against them. If the defendants were Catholics the prosecution would also challenge

Catholic jurors because they might be biased in favour of the defendants. This tended to result in largely Protestant jurors which contributed to the bias. It was at first accepted that it was dangerous to ask Catholics to sit on the jury bench if they lived in areas from which the Provisional IRA operated. The fear of intimidation spread soon to Protestant areas also. As this fear was seen not to be groundless—one person was shot dead in front of his family when it was known that he was about to give incriminating evidence in Court—it became well nigh impossible to operate the judiciary system according to accepted British principles.

This placed William Whitelaw and the Northern Ireland Office in a difficult position: on the one hand internment without trial was repugnant and required that Great Britain enter a derogation against one of the clauses of the European Convention on Human Rights, yet on the other hand the possibility of obtaining convictions against men of violence was being denied to them.

The answer was to appoint a commission of four men, one of whom, a judge, Lord Diplock, was Chairman. They were charged to look into the question of legal procedure in the face of terrorist activities. They were appointed on 18 October 1972 and got down to the job right away, coming forward in December 1972 with the following conclusions:

— that intimidation of witnesses and their families was such that no altering of the normal process of judicial law would suffice. There had to be some form of extra-judicial process. Suspects for a list of scheduled offences, i.e. terrorist-type offences, should be tried by a judge of the High or County Court—sitting alone without any jury and with the usual rights of appeal.
— The armed services should have power to arrest people and to detain them for up to four hours to establish identity. Bail should only be granted by the High Court and then only if certain stringent requirements were met.
— Confessions should be accepted, unless they were obtained by 'torture, inhuman or degrading treatment'. It was left to the judge to determine what was or was not a reasonable interrogation. If explosive matter or firearms were found in a person's car or home, then the onus was on him to prove his innocence, e.g. that he did not know of their presence. Signed witnesses' statements should be accepted for prosecution.

Other recommendations were made for those under 17.[7]

It was agreed to accept these proposals and they were embodied in the Northern Ireland (Emergency Provisions) Act 1973. There had been some question as to whether the army had been acting legally under the Special Powers Act. The Act was superseded by an Order in Council in November 1972 allowing the army or police to hold suspects for 48 hours after which they had to be set free, sent for trial, interned, or served with an Interim Custom Order for 28 days. In the Act of 1973 suspects could be held for 72 hours. The 1974 Prevention of Terrorism (Temporary Provisions) Act, a Westminster Act in answer to the IRA bombing in Birmingham, applied to the whole of the UK and allowed suspects to be held for 48 hours, after which, on a formal consent of the British Home Secretary or the Secretary of State for Northern Ireland they could be held for a further five days.

Special Category Status

Since the organised activity of the Provisionals there have been and still are two general schools of thought on Northern Ireland's problems. One is first to establish peace so that a political solution can be worked out freed from the tensions of violence; the other approach says that the political solution must be found first before one can tackle the question of violent activity. It will be remembered that William Whitelaw was seeking to find some agreement with the Provisionals so that they would call off their campaign. This year 1972 was by far the worst experienced in Northern Ireland (see Appendix C). The bombing campaign was causing serious and costly damage in Belfast, Londonderry and to a lesser extent in other provincial towns. For the first and only occasion more people were killed during the year by political activity than were killed on the roads, 472 as against 372 who lost their lives in road accidents. For the 13 short days of the IRA truce there was a much more happy and free feeling on the streets of Belfast.

It was because of these negotiations that William Whitelaw agreed (it is said also in the face of a threatened hunger strike) that those apprehended with or without trial be given special category status. The people were permitted to wear their own clothes, live in association with their own fellow internees, receive more visits and parcels than the normal offenders, and were not required to do prison work. They could partake of recreational, craft and general educational facilities if they wished.

More facilities were provided at Long Kesh, soon to be called the Maze Prison, and the Special Category prisoners whether convicted or interned were housed in compounds. They were left to work out their way of life and the prison staff usually dealt with the compound's own appointed leader. The warden handed in their food but entered the compounds otherwise only to lock up at night or to make a search or general check.

The Special Category Status applied to all who were accepted as having carried out their lawbreaking act 'for the cause' and this included a number of 'Protestants', who in this connection should be more accurately known as Loyalists. Thus, small numbers of UVF found themselves in one compound and the UDA members, whose numbers were larger, in another. It would have been interesting to have seen what would have happened if they had all been put into the one large compound. The authorities doubtless feared a riot if this had been done and so groups were carefully segregated.

The prison population in Northern Ireland (after the last detainee had been released in 1962, at the end of the IRA's 1956–62 campaign) was about 400. In keeping with the Western European trend, crime increased and by 1968 the numbers had crept up to about 700. Most of these were male and in the Belfast Crumlin Road jail. There was a tiny handful of women in the Armagh jail. By 1972 the daily average of all incarcerated for all reasons had reached 1,500 and by 1974 2,500, around which figure it has tended to remain.

The breakdown of the various types of prisoners in the Maze in the summer of 1974 is given below.

Detainees	Republican	380
Interim custody	Republican	156
Detainees	Loyalist	12
Interim custody	Loyalist	39
Special Category	Republican	481
Special Category	Loyalist	280
On remand	Republican	69
On remand	Loyalist	33
Young prisoners		90
		1,540[9]

As none of the Republicans or Loyalists at this time were required to work, some 90 ordinary young prisoners were brought in to take on various tasks about the prison.

There are further sub-divisions to the above. The Republicans consist both of Official IRA, the original group aiming at an all-Ireland Workers' Republic (a small number) and Provisional IRA (a much larger group) who are housed in separate compounds. The Loyalists might be members of the UDA or UVF. To this were added at a somewhat later date members of other splinter Loyalist groups, such as the Ulster Freedom Fighters or the Red Hand Commandos.

To the Republican Groups were added members of the Irish Republican Socialist Party and the Irish National Liberation Army. It is reported that the UVF on the one side and the Official IRA (and IRSP) on the other are Marxist in thought and will communicate with each other. The Provisionals and the UDA have little except their condition of incarceration in common.

In view of the terrible bombings and murders there was little sympathy for the prisoners—except among the extreme Republicans and Loyalists. There was a certain feeling that the conditions were too easy. A letter in the

Belfast Telegraph from someone who said he was English noted the good chances in the prison to learn a craft or to follow an Open University course while living free off the state, and enquired whether the entrance conditions to the prison were very stringent!

This was not the opinion of many in the prison and living rather as in a prisoner of war camp gave the inmates plenty of opportunity through association to plan various campaigns. One was put into operation in October 1974 when a large section of the prison was burnt down. It was surprising that in spite of all the resultant confusion, no one escaped on this occasion from the Maze prison. Until the huts could be replaced the prisoners had, more or less, to camp out, being protected from the weather by hastily erected plastic sheeting.

The fire was caused by Republicans but the next year there was a Loyalist riot when these prisoners claimed they had been beaten up by prison officers.

By now the Conservative Government was out of office. Merlyn Rees had replaced William Whitelaw and the New Northern Ireland Assembly and Power-Sharing Executive had come and gone.

The Secretary of State had to take over full control again and give a new guidance to another Committee of Seven, under the chairmanship of Lord Gardiner, which was asked to look at the whole question of terrorism, the provision for the administration of justice, to examine the working of the Northern Ireland (Emergency Provisions) Act 1973 and to make recommendations.

The Committee worked on the assumption that Northern Ireland would remain a part of the United Kingdom for the foreseeable future, whatever form devolution might take. The security of the Province was therefore the responsibility of the Government of the UK. Northern Ireland is not a homogeneous society, and the normal conventions of majority rule will not work. No political framework, they maintained, could endure unless both communities share in the responsibility of administering Northern Ireland and recognition is given 'to the different national inheritances of the two communities'.

The Committee satisfied itself that the 1973 Act was not in breach of international agreements. It was held reasonable that the UK derogated from its obligations to preserve liberty, to intern without trial under exceptional circumstances. The members thought that internment had to continue for the time being but imposed on the government the responsibility of ending this detention with trial as soon as the level of violence would allow.

Trial by jury remained the best form of trial (the members maintained), but at present the courts should proceed as recommended by the Diplock Committee. It was recommended that the admissibility of written statements in the Diplock Courts should be ended. Interestingly, it was recommended that it should be a summary offence for editors, printers or publishers of newspapers to take any advertisement from an illegal organisation or part of it. Further, the BBC and Independent Broadcasting Authority were asked to look again at their policy regarding terrorist organisations and the reporting of their activities and policies.

The most important recommendation was that the Special Category Status should be done away with. Its introduction, the members felt, had been a serious mistake, one which William Whitelaw himself was to regret publicly as a serious error of judgement. The category itself appeared to give some official credence to the argument that the political situation justified the action taken. But murder is murder, the Committee maintained, no matter for what cause it is carried out. It should also be made clear, the Committee stated, that the sentences would have to be carried out and that there would be no amnesty.[10]

The Gardiner Report was submitted in January 1975, the Diplock Courts had been in operation since 19 October 1973, the bombing campaign had ceased from its 1972 peak and by 1974 the civil disturbance deaths had fallen from 467 to 216 in the year.

The end of Special Category Status

Merlyn Rees decided the time had come to phase out internment without trial and the last internee was released by the end of 1975.

He also thought in terms of accepting the Gardiner Committee's recommendation to end the Special Category Status. It had been found that the men in this category had been living in the compounds rather as a military unit of their organisation preparing for the time when an amnesty would be granted. Searches had revealed weapons and wooden mock-ups which could be used for training. If prisoner of war status had been agreed to for such special category men they would not be covered by the Geneva Convention,[11] and without uniform on the streets they could be dealt with as the Germans did with the French Resistance.

In the summer of 1975 Merlyn Rees, to encourage good behaviour in the light of the new provisions to come, decided that the normal one third remission of sentence in Great Britain would, in Northern Ireland, be increased to one half. Lord Gardiner had already noted that the law in Northern Ireland gives greater protection to the accused than in most disturbed communities.[12]

The date chosen to end Special Category Status was for those convicted and apprehended after March 1976 for an offence committed after February 1976. New cells had been built at the Maze prison by this time. They were built in the shape of an H, with cells down the long arms and dining hall, wash and toilet accommodation together with offices in the cross section—hence the name 'H' block. They were in keeping with the latest prison design and could not be bettered in Europe. There were eight H blocks, each equipped to take 100 people.

The newly convicted non-special category prisoners were not impressed by this. Due to legal delays the first such did not arrive until near the end of 1976. Soon a protest was set up—they refused to work, they refused to wear prison clothes. They claimed they were not criminals, they did what they did for Ireland. It was an obvious fact that they had not been given a trial by jury, as had the normal criminal, and many would not be in prison but for the political situation. Messrs Boyle, Hadden, and Hillyard made a careful systematic study of the Diplock Court results for 1975 and again for 1979. They found that in 1975 55% of the Republicans and 39% of the Loyalists had no previous record. By 1979 the respective figures were 43% and 14%. By this time the main Loyalist 'offensive' had been called off and their operators (fewer in number represented) rather older and hardened types operating through splinter groups. In 1975 the investigators found that in 1975 no less than 70% of the Republican prisoners were under 21! This was very much the pattern. Young men were recruited from school days and initiated gradually into deeds of violence. The planners (the 'Godfathers' as they came to be called) stayed safely in the background. They had funds behind them; something between £500,000 and £600,000 was collected through robberies, often of banks, and to this had to be added the funds from abroad and protection rackets at home. The Loyalists share in these figures also but to a lesser degree. Some Loyalists also protested against the new provisions.

The position was therefore that one group was claiming special privileges for bombing and shooting in order to do away with a political boundary, while another group was claiming similar privileges when taking violent action to maintain that political boundary. It would be a completely Gilbertian situation for a state to grant special privileges and thereby accord some official endorsement to two illegal private armies with diametrically opposed aims, endangering the lives of citizens, causing very costly property destruction and generally disrupting the state!

Problems of interrogation

Before turning to the history of the protest it is helpful to look at the question of interrogation as this subject is not unrelated.

The Gardiner Committee noted that following the Compton and Parker Reports the number of complaints against the police fell off in 1973 and 1974. Two new interrogation centres were specially built, one at the Gough Army Barracks in Co. Armagh and the other at the main Belfast area police headquarters at Castlereagh. The Diplock Courts convicted on confessions in more than 50% of the cases (56% January–April 1979) for both Republican and Loyalist trials and so there was considerable pressure on the police to obtain a confession. The RUC was also building up a large computerised dossier and suspects were useful at times in giving leads even if it was obvious that they themselves were not connected with any of the paramilitary organisations. The levels of violence (see Appendix C) had fallen very considerably by 1977 and 1978. Roy Mason, who took over towards the end of 1976 as Secretary of State, set store by the number of convictions obtained.

The numbers of complaints of ill-treatment were growing year by year, and some were too well documented to be written off as exaggerated or self-inflicted for propaganda purposes.

Amnesty International do not normally support prisoners who are violent or who operate for a paramilitary organisation. Where there is alleged torture that is a different matter and it was for this reason that they sent an international team to investigate the interrogation methods in Northern Ireland in November 1977. In May 1978 they felt justified through their findings in calling upon the British Government to set up an investigation.

This was agreed to and in June 1978 Judge Bennett and two others were appointed to inquire into police interrogation procedures in Northern Ireland.

The Committee noted that the police had powers to arrest under two Acts. Under the Prevention of Terrorism (Temporary Provisions) Act 1976, a constable had to be 'reasonably' sure that the suspect was connected with terrorist offences. These were broadly defined. The suspect could then be held for not more than 48 hours for questioning, although a warrant to extend this period for a further five days could be obtained from the Secretary of State, a right the Committee was assured was not automatically given. This was a United Kingdom Act first passed in 1974 to deal with IRA activity in England and to exclude suspect characters from entering the country. It also applied to people coming from Northern Ireland to Great Britain and could require those of Northern Ireland birth to be sent back to the Province, provided they had not lived in Great Britain for more than 20 years.

In 1973 the Northern Ireland (Emergency Provisions) Act did not use the word 'reasonably' as an initial arrest requirement. Under this Act the army was also given the right of arrest but could hold a suspect for only four hours before handing him over to the police. In 1978 an amended Act permitted a person to be held for 72 hours following the initial arrest.

There was a set of Judges' Rules made in Great Britain in 1964 (officially adopted for Northern Ireland in October 1976) which stated that any confession to a crime must not have been obtained 'by fear or prejudice or hope of advantage, exercised or held out by a person in authority or by oppression'. In the Diplock Courts a number of confessions had been turned down as inadmissible by the judges. When internment was still in operation, on occasions the police, having failed to obtain a conviction by an admission of guilt, re-arrested the discharged suspect on his leaving the Court and sent him forward for detention. This practice caused bad feeling and did not enhance the gaining of trust in the judicial procedure.

The Bennett Committee made a number of observations and recommendations, the salient ones being that all suspects should have the absolute right to see their solicitor after 48 hours following arrest. It was the law that any person should have the right to see his solicitor provided that this would cause 'no unreasonable delay or hindrance in the process of investigation or the administration of justice'. In practice this had been stretched to cover the entire interrogation period in most cases.

The Committee appreciated that there was 'a co-ordinated and extensive campaign to discredit the RUC', which had a much more difficult task than the police force in any other part of the UK. Any misconduct on the part of the police strengthened the hands of their adversaries. The Committee found the weight of evidence showed that injuries had been sustained during interrogation which could not have been self-inflicted. It was possible that at times the suspect might have to be forcibly restrained, but to minimise any misconduct on the part of the interrogators it was recommended that internal television (vision only) be installed in all rooms used for questioning and that this should be monitored by a uniformed police officer.

The number of detective officers questioning should be limited to two at a time and not more than six should be used on any one case. The interrogations were not to be continued through meal breaks or to continue after midnight. Relatives of suspects frequently did not know what had happened and the Committee requested that the police should re-examine the method by which such information was readily available. Finally large notices explaining the rights of suspects should be displayed in police stations and each suspect (or prisoner) should be given a copy. These recommendations were accepted by the Government and have been put into practice in the main by the police. As a result there was a noticeable falling-off of numbers coming before the Police Complaints Board to complain of the violent handling of suspects before and during interrogation. This independent Government-appointed Board was set up by the Police (Northern Ireland) Order 1977, and followed the setting up of a similar Board in England and Wales. By statute the Board can only act in cases of disciplinary complaints. If the complaints involve allegations deemed to be in breach of the criminal law then these have to be referred to the Director of Public Prosecutions who has the right to decide whether a prosecution in the criminal courts should be undertaken. It is at times a nice point into which category a complaint falls. In the first three years of operation 4,130 complaints were referred to the Board by the police, of which 32% were subsequently withdrawn. It is usually difficult to obtain evidence; many complainants refuse to come forward to give evidence, presumably because they fear that this will put them in bad odour with the police.

In 1980, the fourth year of operation, there were 1,489 cases referred to the Board, containing 1,641 items of complaint. Some 722 were later withdrawn and finally 658 cases were investigated during the year. Of these 575 (87.4%) were criminal offences, but only 13 resulted in prosecutions. In the case of disciplinary offences the Senior Deputy Chief Constable deals with these through his own tribunal, but the Board can over-rule this and request its own tribunal, comprising two Board members and the Senior Deputy Chief Constable. One such instance arose in 1980.[14]

The Board's methods and lack of power have been criticised (as in England) in that it relies on the police to undertake investigations against fellow-policemen. The result of the UK investigation into the matter is awaited, but there is a difficulty particularly in Northern Ireland; the police operate in very dangerous situations. Since 1969 over 140 have been killed and many more seriously injured in the course of their duty. Not only is a strong internal discipline required, but it is essential to maintain a high morale. Outside investigators could have a detrimental effect. It might, however, be possible to effect a compromise and have an ombudsman type of organisation to which complaints could be referred in the first instance.

There still remains the need to obtain a statement of guilt on which so many of the Diplock Court convictions are made. This method of conviction is, according to Lord Gardiner's 1975 report, a second best forced on the community by the violent situation. In June 1981 a group of individuals concerned with peacemaking and the achievement of individual liberty and public security in Northern Ireland held a conference in Belfast, to which Lord Gardiner came as chairman. The whole question of the administration of justice in Northern Ireland was reviewed. In a comprehensive survey it was suggested that a number of offences now termed 'schedule' acts of violence might well be dealt with under normal Court rules, offences, that is, which bore a relatively short prison sentence.

The conference passed a resolution unanimously calling for a new official review on the lines of the Gardiner Committee of 1975. An ad hoc group was formed in the summer of 1981 to undertake this work.

The prison protest

The protesting prisoners were in the meantime refusing to wear prison clothes and draped themselves in blankets. They claimed they were denied the statutory hour's exercise each day because the prison authorities said that blankets must not be taken out of the cells. They refused to exercise in the nude or in sports wear supplied by the prison, though they did wear prison issue if they wished to claim their monthly visit from relatives. They also put on trousers to go to Mass or another form of church service.

There were a few Loyalist prisoners also 'on the blanket' as it was called. Not all those convicted after March 1976 went on the blanket, but by 1980 there were some 300 protesting in this manner and they occupied three of the eight 'H' blocks.

As they were not making any headway with this protest they decided in March 1978 to smash up furniture and the windows and to refuse to 'slop out', smearing the excrement on the walls of the cells. This was used for propaganda purposes, particularly in the United States of America, where among those of Irish stock it was represented as a policy of the wicked British who kept men locked up in these foul conditions. The protesting prisoners were in practice moved into clean cells every ten days or so and the dirty cells were cleaned with steam-cleaning equipment. The prisoners were also required to have a bath, to which, on occasions, they objected. They would then start again to foul up their new clean cells. They were monitored carefully by the medical services but their health remained persistently good.

In 1979 an application was made on behalf of four of the protesting prisoners to the European Commission on Human Rights. It was alleged that their treatment was in breach of a number of clauses of the European Convention on Human Rights. The Commission, reporting on 15 May 1980, found that 'the applicants are attempting to achieve a status of political prisoner which they are not entitled to under national law or under the Convention'. The protest could not be attributed to any positive action of the British Government and was done to obtain maximum publicity for their cause . . . 'these conditions are self-imposed by the applicants as part of their protest'. They could take exercise and use the library facilities if they so wished.

At the same time the Commission was concerned 'at the inflexible approach of the State authorities which has been concerned more to punish offenders than to explore ways of resolving such a serious deadlock'.

Before the Report was published the Northern Ireland Office had already made some concessions. Four letters a month could be sent and received instead of one, an extra visit a month could be had in addition to the statutory monthly visit. Sports wear could be worn during recreation time, which had been extended, and there was some opportunity of association with other prisoners in the evening. Later in October it was agreed that prison uniform would be abolished and would be replaced by civilian-type clothing.

The hunger strike and its effects

The protesters were not making the progress they hoped for in regaining political status, and on 27 October 1980 seven men refused food and went on hunger strike, taking only water. As Christmas approached and 53 days had elapsed, they were in a weak condition. An official of the Northern Ireland Office visited them in the prison hospital and explained the concessions. One of their number lapsed into unconsciousness and the others asked for medical treatment and commenced taking nourishment themselves. There was enough in the concessions to claim in the meantime a victory.

It was then found that there was to be no liberal interpretation of the rules—work had to be done according to the dictates of the prison staff and although civilian-type clothing could be worn it had to be prison-issued clothes during work periods. There had been enough possible misunderstandings for the prisoners to claim they had been misled and four men again went on hunger strike.

The death of Frank McManus, the Republican elected to Westminster for the Fermanagh-South Tyrone constituency, necessitated a by-election. Provisional Sinn Fein nominated one of the hunger strikers, Bobby Sands, for the seat. The SDLP were going to contest this division but decided not to become involved in splitting up the Catholic vote and withdrew their candidate. This had the effect of leaving the election on 9 April 1981 as a straight alternative between a Provisional IRA man convicted of attempted murder and the former Unionist Party leader at Stormont, Harry West. In this area there are no floating voters; it was a question of how many Catholics would abstain. There was an 86% poll and Bobby Sands in his sixth week without food was elected on 9 April by a 1,446 majority out of 62,818. There were 3,280 spoiled votes, almost certainly for the most part from Catholics. Even though they may have deplored the acts of Bobby Sands it was too much to ask of many Catholics that they should vote Unionist—and for such an obvious Unionist of the traditional mould.

Naturally the Provisionals were able to claim this result as a great victory. Who again dare say that only a tiny minority of Catholics supported them? The eventual death of Bobby Sands on 5 May led to some considerable rioting, though this was confined to Catholic areas (particularly Belfast) and directed against the security forces, who literally drew their fire and prevented a violent clash with Loyalist groups. There was in Belfast a marked contrast between the Catholic areas of the West and North, littered with the well-known post-riot debris of burned-out vehicles and broken glass, and the Protestant areas, carrying wall graffiti 'Let Bobby Sands die', where life went on more or less unaffected—not entirely unaffected, for there was another hardening of attitudes and the re-polarisation of thought. The District Council elections which took place in May 1981 were conducted in this emotive setting. The result was that votes went in favour of hard-line candidates, particularly on the Protestant side, and reasonable liberals of, for instance, the Alliance Party, were the consequent sufferers.

As the summer months of 1981 passed so other hunger strikers died, three more in May, two in July, and another four in August. As they died others came forward to take their places, refusing food and taking only water.

The tenth man died on 17 August 1981, just four days before the polling day in the by-election to fill the seat at Westminster vacant since the death of Bobby Sands. His election agent, Owen Carron, announced that he would stand as an 'Anti-H Block' candidate, pledged to carry on with the campaign for political status. He was opposed by an Official Unionist, Kenneth Maginnis. The SDLP again refused to nominate a candidate, but there were two others who might attract Catholic votes: Seamus Close, for the Alliance Party, and Tom Moore, for the Republican Clubs Workers' Party, a non-violent socialist group.

Owen Carron was returned with a majority larger than at the previous by-election, 2,230 over the Unionist candidate, with a slightly increased poll, 88.2%. The Alliance candidate polled 1,930 votes, and the Republican Workers' Party candidate only 1,132—both losing their deposits. As the number of spoiled votes almost vanished, it looked as though these had gone this time to these two candidates, the emotional support arising from the deaths of ten young men being too strong to draw other votes away from Carron.

For some years the Provisionals had tended to disappear from the general activities in Catholic areas. They operated an underground cellular campaign; people were no longer sure who was and who was not a member. However, with the great morale boost from these two elections, coupled with reports of increased support from Irish-Americans and increased funds for their Noraid fund for Northern Ireland, the Provisionals began again to exert some overt pressure in Catholic areas. Community leaders and those Catholics working for an end to the violence were thus placed under considerable strain.

Protestants were irritated by what they saw as murderers trying to gain sympathy by using political blackmail and they hoped that the Northern Ireland Office would not give way. Reasonable Protestants were concerned, along with reasonable Catholics, to try to find some formula short of granting political status which would open the way to stop this sad and senseless loss of life. It was hoped that the Catholic church leaders would make a strong appeal. This was in fact made by bishops and by the Cardinal himself, and they were accompanied by an appeal to the Northern Ireland Office to be 'more flexible' in their interpretation of the prison rules. This request was always left vague and it was not clear whether the hunger strikers would, in fact, accept any conditions short of granting their 'five demands'.[15] Several bodies tried to act as intermediaries, in particular the representatives of the Irish Commission for Justice and Peace, who proposed that prisoners should be allowed to wear their own clothes at all times, that they should have increased opportunities for association with other prisoners, and that they should be given work to do which was of some cultural or educative value. It was not clear whether the hunger strikers would accept these conditions. In any case Humphrey Atkins, the Secretary of State, made it clear that the Government would not act under duress. If the strikers ended their fast he would then clarify what would happen. There would be further developments for all prisoners.

Meanwhile it was clear that a number of relatives of the hunger strikers were no longer behind the action as had been the families of the earlier strikers. On 30 July a number of relatives called on the Provisional IRA to order an end to the campaign. The next day the relatives of one of the hunger strikers called on the prison hospital staff to give resuscitation to the man in question, Patrick Quinn, when he fell into a coma.

During the next two months families intervened on four occasions to save the lives of hunger strikers. Denis Faul, a priest who had for a number of years been active in reporting over-reaction and malpractices by the security forces, and was in favour of the campaign for political status, nevertheless became prominent in support of the action of the relatives in their intervention. Finally on 3 October the hunger strike action was called off. It was thought that the Provisionals were probably glad to terminate a campaign which, though gaining them much support, had by this time become counter-productive with men going on and coming off the fast.

By ending the strike the Provisionals indirectly saved the life of Alan Human, an Oxford graduate born in South Africa, who had been fasting outside the Belfast City Hall for 26 days. Though of South African parentage he had been educated in England since he was 12, and had been living in the Republic of Ireland. He felt called upon to make this lonely vigil, unto death if necessary, in a bid to end the Maze hunger strike.

The Secretary of State announced that all prisoners, of all types, in Northern Ireland, would henceforth be allowed to wear their own clothes, and that if they conformed to prison rules could retain 50% of the good conduct remission of sentence which they had previously earned. Some 300 men decided that they would continue the protest by refusing to work. Even they were allowed to qualify for one half of the 50% period of remission. The 50% remission facility had led prisoners in Great Britain, where one third remission is the rule, to request equal treatment with Northern Ireland prisoners. The sad and tragic position remains that some 1,600 men and approaching 100 women are deprived of their freedom because of their part in the violence. A considerable proportion are serving long sentences. Some prisoners are the type of person from whom society would in any case require protection. The majority, however, would not be there had they not been motivated by a spirit of nationalism, whether for 'Ireland' or for 'Ulster', which led them directly or indirectly to commit terrible acts.

For those who maintain that the means shape the ends, and that the more laudable and desirable the aim, the more impossible its attainment becomes through harmful means, acts of destruction of property and above all, of life, are therefore quite unequivocally immoral. Most people, however, maintain that citizens of a nation are justified, indeed required, at times to support violent means to defend the state. One then has to define what is meant by 'the state' which it is argued, legitimises, under certain circumstances, the use of violence. Would the majority of the citizens of Northern Ireland ever be justified in taking up arms to preserve the British link, or to gain independence of government?

One of the requirements of the Church's theory of the 'just war' is that all non-violent means of redressing grievances must have been exhausted. This is clearly not the case in Northern Ireland. Further, although in numerous places in the world one man's 'terrorists' are another's 'freedom fighters', in Northern Ireland (notwithstanding the results of the summer by-elections of 1981) it is clear that only a tiny proportion of the population approves the acts of violence on either side.

5 Living in a violent community

The effect of violence in Northern Ireland on each individual depends very much on where he lives, which in turn is largely governed by who he is and by his socio-economic standing. For those fortunate enough to live in a relatively safe area, the 'troubles' may be only an annoying irritant to the usual problems of 'keeping up with the Jones'' in modern western society. For anyone, however, who has had a loved one shot, who has had both legs blown off in an explosion, or finds her husband serving a life sentence, life can never be the same again. The effects of the violence are not confined to Northern Ireland alone, for there are the relatives of the 350 soldiers who have lost their lives as well as those who have been killed in bomb blasts in England and in the Republic of Ireland.

Obviously the burden of violence is never equally shared. Although reasonable compensation is paid by the UK exchequer against malicious damage claims, how can one assess the value of a limb, or the strain of building up a business again after the premises have been wrecked? No compensation is given to those whose shop or business has lost trade and had to close down because of the rioting and the violence. An elderly person whose home has been burnt can never be fully compensated by the current market value of the contents. In the eighties problems of bomb damage have been largely superseded by those caused by major factory closures and redundancies of the trade recession.

The irritations and inconveniences, however, are shared by all. Practices that once would have seemed intolerable soon become accepted as normal. These comprise friskings and bag searches when entering the shopping area of Belfast, some form of security check on shops and offices, spot checks by police or army on the roads, diversions due to bombs or bomb scares and the consequent traffic delays on certain routes, delaying people going to work and getting home in the evening. During these years there were frequent bomb scares when offices and factories had to be evacuated. Even schoolchildren tired of this novel break from classes. There are large areas in Belfast when during the day a vehicle must not be left unattended. Quite a sizeable proportion of those working in Londonderry, Belfast and a number of provincial towns must, at some time or other, have taken part in a clearing up operation, if only of shattered glass.

There was a time when it was deemed sufficient to require travellers by air to identify their baggage as they stepped on to the plane. This practice was changed to the more intensive search still carried out today. Not only does this involve arriving early to allow for a time-consuming luggage search, but it also adds to the fare of the journey as security costs must be met.

It is obligatory to have a security man on the door of all buildings entered by the public. He should have a warning bell push or siren horn near at hand, but it is an accepted fact that even so he cannot be expected to prevent the man with a gun from entering the building. Statutory grants are available to meet the security man's wages; this is yet another item in the cost to the nation of civil disturbances. There are now many men and women for whom 'peace' would probably mean the loss of employment.

Although it is to man's advantage to be so adaptable as to be able to ride out the storm, it is quite horrifying to realise how soon one can become almost immune to the surrounding trauma of tragedy and death. The relentless repetition of violence and tragedy over the years can all too easily become accepted as the norm. Frequent public condemnations of violence, calls to repentance, and days of prayer themselves, in turn, generate indifference. The public fast as a method of reawakening public conscience has been sullied as has been mentioned by the action of the Provisional IRA hunger strikers. The reconciling organisations thus turn to more positive schemes and accept gratefully that in spite of all the terrible happenings there is so much kindness and human decency around.

That these decencies can be maintained in the ghetto areas or segregated housing estates is creditable for it is here that most of the violence takes place. It has been the experience of the writer with the Belfast Voluntary Welfare Society that the majority of those coming for help to this longstanding social service agency have been affected by the civil disturbances at a level deeper than those listed as irritating or frustrating. Probably they will fall into one or more of these categories:

1. Some member of the family will have been killed or in some way physically injured.
2. Some members of the family will be or will have been in prison for a sectarian offence.
3. The client will have had to move home because of intimidation.
4. The breadwinner will have had to give up his job because of threats or even because he was fearful of crossing a territory of the opposite side, having been badly beaten up so doing.
5. The client has been 'bad with my nerves' because of rioting and violence.
6. The client is deeply worried because her son has been caught up with a paramilitary group.

These facts need not form the overt problem, but they will be a complicating factor. Rather sad exceptions are where the women have felt constrained to say of husbands or sons in prison 'at least he is safer in there, he won't get shot', or more frequently the wife admits that with her husband in prison she is better off than before as the social security amounts to more than her husband gave her each week, from earnings often not disclosed to the wife. Finance is an ever present problem, increasingly so as unemployment soars and with the cost of fuel escalating, many families find it harder and harder to keep out of debt.

Such experiences are in marked contrast to those who form the executive committees of voluntary bodies operating across the broad spectrum of social service. Drawn for the most part from the professional or managerial socio-economic groups, they do not live in riot areas or on housing estates that harbour gunmen; they may never have met a member of a paramilitary organisation. They do not have their houses searched by the army. They are not held by the RUC for questioning. The wives are not required to bang their metal dustbin lids on the pavement in protest against the army and they are not worried lest their children are enticed into a terrorist group, nor do they find that pressure is put upon them to subscribe to some thinly disguised paramilitary victims' fund. They may, however, have had their places of work bombed and had to face the problems of new premises and general re-establishment. The Belfast Welfare Society has had the windows of its headquarters blown in on five occasions.

No-one, of course, is completely invulnerable. A former member of the Executive Committee of this Society, a Catholic, had the misfortune to have her house maliciously destroyed by fire, though she lived in a middle class area. A former member of the Northern Ireland Council of the Social Service Executive Committee and a former Senator had her home attacked by two gunmen. Her husband in trying to prevent their entry was wounded, though not seriously, by the ensuing shot and, the alarm having been given, the men made off.

It is not always possible to know whether such a hold-up was on behalf of a political group or someone acting on his own. In 1972, the most violent year, there were in the Province as a whole 1,931 armed robberies from banks, post offices and businesses amounting to £790,000.[1] Prior to 1968 Northern Ireland was relatively free from crime compared with Great Britain and elsewhere. Like everywhere else crime increased and the prison population crept up from 479 in 1948 to 727 in 1968. The big rise to nearly 3,000 by the late seventies was almost entirely due to the Republicans' campaign of violence and its Loyalist counterpart in opposition.

It is a complicated task trying to unravel the pattern of violence and murder on either side. The targets change; splinter groups are involved. In contrast to the worldwide assassination attempts on the lives of world figures it almost appears as if there were some form of tacit agreement not to shoot the leaders on either side in Northern Ireland. The judiciary and leading members of the Government are given a modicum of security protection, but it is impossible to give everyone at risk complete protection all round the clock. The list of exceptions grows. The shooting of Robert Bradford MP is dealt with on page 41. This assassination had considerable repercussions. It came at the end of a week of killings and was seen as a direct threat to the Protestant community. John D. Taylor, the Unionist Minister of Home Affairs at Stormont 1970–72, and one of the current members of the European Parliament, was shot at in Armagh City in 1972. His jaw bone was shattered and he was fortunate, with the help of plastic surgery, to make a good recovery.

Jack Barnhill, a Unionist Senator from 1958 to 1971, was assassinated at his home near Strabane in December 1971. The Official IRA claimed responsibility for these murders, but said that they only wished to destroy his home because the army has destroyed working class homes. He was, however, killed in a struggle.

On the other side of the divide a small group calling themselves the Ulster Freedom Fighters stabbed to death a Catholic Senator, G. Paddy Wilson, in a roadside quarry in the hills to the North of Belfast. A member of the SDLP, he was to the left of the Party and at the time of his death he had been acting as an election agent in the Northern Ireland Assembly elections for Gerry Fitt MP. A woman to whom he had given a lift in his car was also killed. Paddy Wilson had always refused to carry a gun. Gerry Fitt himself claims that he saved his own life by holding an IRA group at bay by brandishing a gun from the stairs of his home.

Maire Drumm who had resigned from the chairmanship of Sinn Fein was murdered in hospital. It was presumed that this was by an extreme Loyalist group, but there was some doubt about it.

At Westminster Airey M. S. Neave, the Conservative spokesman on Northern Ireland, was killed by a car bomb as he left the House of Commons in March 1979. His murder was claimed by a Republican splinter group, the Irish National Liberation Army. Prior to this death Christopher Ewart-Biggs, the British Ambassador to the Republic of Ireland, was killed when a land mine blew up his car near his home just outside Dublin. A young woman civil servant was killed with him. His wife, Jane Ewart-Biggs, said that she felt no bitterness towards the Irish people. She joined the Peace People and continues to be a good friend of Northern Ireland.

Finally, there was the Mountbatten family tragedy, when the Earl's yacht was blown up in August 1979 off the coast of County Sligo. Those who caused this callous and cowardly deed must have been quite indifferent to the numbers who lost their lives. Two other members of the family together with a local boatman died. The event was an acute embarrassment to the Dublin Government—an elderly soldier and statesman of international renown had chosen their country as a place where he was happy to spend at least part of his time.

At one period during the mid-seventies one or two businessmen were murdered. There was a rumour that the Provisional IRA had a list of 50 leading Ulster industrialists and that they were going to pick them off one by one. This did not happen, however. The Provisionals' main targets are army personnel and the members of the Ulster Defence Regiment. The RUC and their reservists and members of the prison service are also included. The Provisionals claim they have no desire to kill Irishmen, but if they serve the security forces then they are working for Britain, the enemy. If others get killed by bomb blast or caught in crossfire, this is an unfortunate fact of warfare. Some attempt is nearly always made to give a warning of a bomb to the public, by phoning the police, the press or the BBC.

At the beginning of the bombing campaign in 1971 each bomb was regarded as being aimed at a specific target for an identifiable reason. It subsequently appeared that the object was to destroy and dislocate life in Northern Ireland, in order that, finding the Province too costly in men and materials, the British would decide to leave. It did not thus matter where the stolen car was left in the city or provincial town so long as its contents caused maximum damage and dislocation. At times lorries have been hi-jacked and the owner told to drive it to a certain location with a bomb on board, his mate being held as a hostage to ensure the orders were correctly carried out. If the bomb maker or carrier is blown up with his own device this is referred to by the security forces, in Association Football jargon, as an 'own goal'.

Loyalist bombs have frequently been aimed at public houses as many of these are Catholic owned. The compliment has naturally been returned. At the time of the Ulster Workers' Council Strike, in May 1974, car bombs exploded without warning in Monaghan and Dublin in the Republic. Five people were killed in the former town and 22 in the city. Many more were injured and three more subsequently died. Both the UDA and the UVF denied responsibility, but three cars were found from Northern Ireland. It was ascertained that they had been hijacked in a Protestant area in Belfast earlier in the day. The victims were ordinary people going home from their day's work, and it is a curious anomaly of the era of violence that this heinous crime generated but little animosity in the Republic either among the general public or at governmental level. Brian Faulkner for the Northern Ireland Assembly sent a message of 'deepest regret' to Liam Cosgrave. The Taoiseach in expressing 'the revulsion and condemnation felt of all in this island' saw fit to note that it helped 'to bring home to us here what the people in Northern Ireland have been suffering for years'.

This heartless disregard for life was repeated—by the IRA—in November of the same year when bombs in two Birmingham public houses killed 19 people and injured 182. The Provisionals claimed they were not involved but on 25 November 1974 the Home Secretary declared the IRA to be an illegal organisation in Great Britain as in Northern Ireland. It was as a result of this event that the Prevention of Terrorism Act was extended to Northern Ireland. Persons could now be held without charge for up to seven days and expulsion of someone to Northern Ireland from Great Britain became legal.

Intimidation has been mentioned. This was a sad and cowardly feature of the early days of violence when people were issued with ugly threats to leave the area just because of religious affiliation. Frequently these threats were made anonymously or by roving gangs and not by the neighbours, where good relationships had been maintained over the years. The first large scale move came after the violence in the summer of 1969 and it was intensified after the post-internment riots of the summer of 1971. By this time no threat could be ignored with impunity. At times friendly neighbours became frightened at the possibility of the house next door being bombed and set alight, and encouraged the neighbours to go. Thus areas of Belfast and of many other towns, where different denominations had mixed harmoniously, became almost completely polarised and segregated. Studies of intimidation were made by the Community Relations Commission culminating in a publication by two research officers of the Commission.[2] No one knows how many people have actually moved their home in Northern Ireland because of civil disturbances, but authors based their estimates on survey studies over a period of three and a half years. Then, after cross-checking with figures obtained from a voluntary body, the Belfast Housing Aid Society, they estimated that in Belfast alone about 15,000 families moved home between August 1969 and February 1973. The average size of the family of the evacuees was found to be four so that something approaching 60,000 individuals were involved in this movement, spanning only a relatively short period of time. The Catholic population of Belfast was 28% but something like 60% of those moving were Catholic. Housing thus became in very short supply in 'safe' Catholic areas but relatively easy to find in Protestant areas. On the dangerous fringe areas houses were abandoned, either bricked up by the housing authorities or owners or they were left to the ravages of the vandals.

The writers of the Survey reported, 'Quietly, unpublicised, lost in the inner pages of newspapers, the largest enforced population movement in Europe since the second world war is going on in Northern Ireland'.[3]

Some individuals and families left Northern Ireland because they were tired of violence, others because they saw no future there for themselves, or more likely for their children. During the worst years of disturbances there was the anxiety—not entirely absent today—that the Province would suffer a severe drain of the enterprising. There was a saying, 'Would the last person to leave Northern Ireland please switch off the light'.

Some, however, really had to get out of the country for their own safety and that of their family. This was recognised by the Department of Health and Social Services, who asked the Belfast Voluntary Welfare Society to administer on its behalf a fund to pay, within limits, the cost of moving the person's furniture to Great Britain. It was not intended to be a cheap method of moving out of Ulster and corroboration was required, from the army or police, that the person should move for his own safety. The conditions are thus fairly stringent and from 1972 to the time of writing under 400 cases have been dealt with. The Voluntary Society has also used private funds to help those who fell just outside the scheme but the numbers involved are still relatively few in number. After a year or so it was noticeable that the intimidation was starting to come from within each community—someone knew too much, or was thought to be a possible informer.

The police urge the use of a confidential telephone number to give information which might lead to the discovery of a bomb 'factory' or the apprehension of a criminal. It is one thing to disapprove of paramilitary action; it is another to inform against your own 'side'. The risk of being an informer cannot be taken lightly. If discovered it may lead to death, or at best, being shot through the legs or knees ('knee-capping')—the traditional punishment of the Provisionals. It can be graded from a flesh wound to permanent laming according to the offence. During times of active Loyalist counter-violence there were reports of some shootings of their own side and of people being badly beaten up as punishment.

Other organisations have helped people to leave areas where they may be drawn into violent activities. Such action may save a young man from being involved with causing the death of others or of wasting years of his life behind prison wires. This task has become more and more difficult as job opportunities in Great Britain disappear.

Legal protection for minorities and for the citizen

As well as making some provision to give the citizen the right to a modicum of redress against police excesses, as in Great Britain, there exists an Ombudsman dealing with complaints against both central government and local authority malfunction.

Where sizeable minorities exist other measures are required. Northern Ireland has no Race Relations Act, but other minority protection laws have been enacted in an attempt to rule out discrimination. There are so few overseas immigrants that the colour question virtually does not exist, but obviously it is another matter when dealing with the Catholic minority.

Much has been written on the subject of discrimination, in the obtaining of jobs and on promotion opportunities—using examples of anti-Catholic bias and demonstrating under-representation on the Catholic side.[4] It is not intended here to go back over this ground except to say, at the risk of over-simplification, that both sides discriminated but as there are more non-Catholic firms or employers Catholics came off worst. This was particularly noticeable in local government where there were only about 11 of the 73 local authorities which were not Unionist controlled. The situation changed with the Local Government Act (N.I.) 1972 when the former system was replaced by 26 local councils, which no longer had the remit to provide schools or houses. Houses were provided centrally by the Housing Executive, formed in 1971, and the education function was in the hands of the central Department of Education, and administered through four Area Boards.

As promised in the O'Neill package deal of reforms in November 1968 an Ombudsman's office was opened in Belfast in July 1969 with the Ombudsman for Great Britain, Sir Edmund Compton, undertaking the task for the initial period. His remit covered Government Ministries only, but in May Chichester-Clark (following O'Neill as Prime Minister) had announced that there would also be an Ombudsman for local councils and public bodies. This facility commenced in December 1969, with an Ulsterman, John Benn, as Commissioner for Complaints, which in fact pre-dated the establishment of a similar office in Great Britain.

At central government level any accepted allegations of maladministration cannot be upheld by the Court judgement, but they are usually capable of adjustment with a reasonable settlement. In his first report in January 1971 Edmund Compton stated that he had investigated 33 complaints made to his office and found that only two were justified. He felt that the Northern Ireland Ministries were able to give better service to citizens than comparable Ministries in Great Britain.

Naturally at local government level there were more complaints, 970 in the first ten months of operation, of which 74 alleged sectarian discrimination. In all John Benn found that in 12 cases there had been injustice to the complainant. The Commissioner for Complaints has, in fact, access to the courts to support his findings if they cannot be settled by agreement. In 1974 the two services were administered from the one office and by the one Commissioner.

Statutory measures had previously been taken to try to curb religious discrimination. Since 1971 Government Ministries (since Direct Rule departments) will not consider tenders from contractors who do not sign a clause agreeing not to practise religious discrimination. This rule also applies to all firms in receipt of Government grants in respect of new buildings and machinery.

In 1973 the Northern Ireland Constitution Act has made it unlawful for public bodies to discriminate against any person on the grounds of religious belief or political opinion and rendered any discriminatory legislation void.

It is not possible to change the nature of a community by means of the statute book. There must in the first place be a majority in any democratic legislature in favour of the change, or the law would not be drafted and enacted. The coming of Direct Rule from Westminster altered the situation somewhat, but by the mid-seventies the climate of opinion in Northern Ireland towards religious discrimination had changed over the previous 20, or even ten years. In the fifties it was said to the writer 'I think each side looks after its own', and in certain firms and some local authorities this was taken for granted. By the seventies, helped no doubt by the reports in the national media, liberal moderate opinion had scored over tribal custom and discrimination on religious grounds was no longer generally acceptable. At least, the practice had to be veiled and more subtle and so it was possible in 1976 for the Northern Ireland Office of the UK Government to augment the existing provisions with a Fair Employment Agency.

This body with a staff of 14 and a nominated Board of 11 members, has a dual function not only of looking into complaints resulting from alleged religious discrimination, but also the positive one of promoting equality of opportunity. It has the power to take cases to the courts, if all else fails, and is also required to carry out research and make investigation without any special complaint being made to it. In pursuit of the aim of promoting equality for all, signatures to a Declaration of Principle and Intent provide equal opportunity for appointment and promotion. About 2,500 have been obtained.

The Agency realises that, particularly in an area of high unemployment, it is time saving, cheap and convenient not to advertise for manual jobs. A note of requirements on the shop floor board, and by word of mouth a supply of workers is on the doorstep the next morning. The writer remembers that when he worked in a linen manufacturing firm, all the laundry workers in the finishing department were Catholic. The manager of the section was a Protestant, not particularly liberal in his views, but when some of the laundry staff heard he wanted another member, they would say, 'I can get you a real good worker'. It was easy—no cost, no bother, and some form of guarantee of good work. Usually this method worked against the Catholic, but in any case to achieve equality of opportunity the Agency requires firms to take positive steps to break down such situations. There is also the danger that if it is known that a firm is almost 100% of one side the other group feels that it is not worth the bother to apply.

This situation has much improved and in the review of the year 1980 the Fair Employment Agency received 43 new complaints, to which 17 pending from the previous year were added. Investigations were completed in 25 of these and only three were deemed to be warranted cases of discrimination. As in the case of race problems it is all too easy to blame rejection on one's race or religious grouping. However, some bad cases still arise. In 1978 the Agency had brought to its notice the case of a Catholic who had worked as a recreation officer for the Craigavon

Borough Council for five years with high commendation. He applied for promotion to a senior officer's position. The job was offered to a Protestant applicant from outside the Council's service who had not the same qualifications or experience. The Agency claimed that this was unlawful discrimination. The Craigavon Borough Council took the case to the Armagh County Court which found in their favour and quashed the Agency's findings. The Agency then decided to take the case to the Court of Appeal and on 30 June 1981 their verdict was upheld in an unanimous judgement. The Agency is claiming compensation for the client who by this time might not want the post.[5]

Discrimination can sometimes work the other way round. Almost all Catholics go to Catholic schools. Their governing bodies would require that most of their teachers should be Catholics. It was thus decided that the question of teaching posts should not be included within the remit of the Fair Employment Act 1976. Catholics can thus apply for teaching posts in state schools where the ruling of the Commissioner for Complaints would apply, but Protestants are not protected in the case of refusal of posts in Catholic schools. The position is under review.

The Commissioner for Complaints has referred complaints of religious discrimination to the Fair Employment Agency since its formation in 1976. Out of the 744 complaints received (in) 1980 the Commissioner for Complaints found only 23 (about 5% of those investigated) where there was actual maladministration. He was able to effect a settlement satisfactory to all parties in some 122 cases including most of the 23 referred to. The majority were complaints against the Northern Ireland Housing Executive covering both Protestants and Catholics and underlying what a great problem council housing is in the Province especially in Belfast. In two cases where settlement could not be effected a hearing with an Education and Library Board and the Housing Executive was held.

An interesting case arose, again with the Craigavon Borough Council. This Council had at first agreed to lease a site to the Catholic Gaelic Football Social and Recreation Club to build a youth club and sports field, a decision they then reversed. The Commissioner thought that the Club had suffered an injustice and that the leases should be granted as originally agreed. The Council later agreed the Commissioner's decision, and granted the leases, whereupon the MP for the area complained to the Commissioner that in assisting the Gaelic Athletic Association, he had extended the influence of a body that actively discriminated against the police and their reserve, the army and the Ulster Defence Regiment! The Commissioner stated that he could not accept this complaint as it was made by an aggrieved person within the meaning of the Act.[6]

The economic factor

The story of life in Northern Ireland would be unbalanced if stress were not laid on the effects of the economic situation. In the minds and lives of so many the problem of making ends meet looms larger than that of violence.

By 1969 the three leading industries, agriculture, textiles and shipbuilding, were only employing a fraction of the numbers in work 20 years earlier.[7] Agriculture was efficient but highly mechanised. The towns could not absorb the flight from the land. The linen industry, in which the Ulsterman had world acknowledged expertise, could not compete in price with man-made fibres, and shipbuilding was obviously in decline, while the aircraft industry was unable to take its place as an employer.

When there was full employment in Great Britain there was an overall unemployment rate in Northern Ireland of between 6% and 8%. Even then the male unemployment rate in places like Londonderry, Newry and Strabane reached 20%. Not to have a job was thus no stigma; social security was an accepted means of livelihood. Northern Ireland cannot afford a Britain in recession. A ready market for Ulster's products—particularly for the British and overseas firms with Northern Ireland branches was of greater significance than the effect of the riot situation. Northern Ireland's productivity increase was certainly at a higher rate than Great Britain's up to 1974.

However, with escalation of costs and, in the eighties, the rapid increase in unemployment almost doubling the GB rate at every stage, poverty in Northern Ireland is becoming a major feature of the scene and is causing hardship.

Affluence and the continual increase in wages clouds the true economic situation for a period. In Northern Ireland the average manual wage was, for a long period, about three-quarters that of Britain. By 1970 the Ulsterman earned on average 78% of the GB figure. By 1978 this figure had reached 89.5%. As against this the size of family in Northern Ireland, again on average, is higher than in the rest of the UK and fuel costs are much higher, with coal 10% more, electricity about 22% higher and in the absence of North Sea Gas, the gas bills are about double. The lowest paid workers are thus at a considerable disadvantage which rent rebates and the Family Income Supplement cannot make up.

A study made in 1978 showed that in workers' housing areas around Belfast, 64% of the households interviewed were living below the short-term supplementary benefit rate plus 40%—the arbitrary level often used in survey to indicate a 'poverty level'.[8] As may be imagined a larger proportion of the population in Northern Ireland is dependent on supplementary benefit than is the case in Great Britain (14% as against 8%).[9]

Socio-economic studies in the Province show Catholics over-represented in the unskilled and semi-skilled groups.[10] They will have more than their expected proportion of unemployed. Although there are more Catholics around with degrees than previously, the average Catholic is still to be found in the semi-skilled group, while the average Protestant will be one group higher up the skilled worker group, i.e. having a trade. Thus he will be more likely to be sought by any new capital intensive high technology firm.

Although, as has been seen, there is no longer the same chance of discrimination in obtaining a job as there would have been in the fifties or even the sixties, the years of violence have left their mark and a man may still be ostracised at his work, or even unofficially threatened if he stays at his job.

In the fifties it was always feared that rioting might break out in factories where both sides would meet and quarrel at work. It has not happened that way, but there has been some added segregation of labour because of the situation of the plant, or factory. Some people dare not pass through certain streets to go to their work. The longstanding linen firm, the Ulster Weaving Company, which gave birth to the famous Linfield Football Club (the Blues) is deep in the ultra-Protestant Sandy Row area. There was a time when no Catholic would go near this district. Then, owing to the influence of the managing director, Sir Graham Larmour, Catholics were encouraged to take jobs in the factory, and by the late fifties this firm had become noted for its mixed and good group relations. In the riots of the seventies the Catholic workers dropped off. This pattern has been repeated elsewhere.

In spite of all the new legislation the 1980 Report of the Fair Employment Agency noted that the occupational gap between the two communities had not narrowed. Absence of discrimination was not enough; a more positive approach was required.[11]

Violence and the social services

In 1971 leaders in the Catholic community, observing that internment was, in practice, for Catholics only, called for the withholding of rent and rates for those in statutory housing as a protest. The Government countered this action with the Payment of Debt (Emergency Provisions) Act in October of that year which provided for the collection of debt from wages paid in the public sector but also, within limits, from social security benefits. In 1972 there were 17,183 tenants on strike of whom 13,299 were paying enforced rent and rates arrears.[12] Pressure to conform to the civil disobedience action eased over the years, particularly in 1974 with the advent of the Power-Sharing Executive. Many of the debts had been cleared by 1976, but by this time electricity debts were mounting in an alarming fashion and it was decided to take powers to include the collection of electricity arrears also. This extension brought Protestants in also. The practice was followed, for habitual non-payers, of deducting the average weekly current cost of electricity as well as a sum towards arrears. Dating from the days of the rent and rates strike no appeal to a tribunal is permitted, but the writer was one of two people in Northern Ireland asked to make recommendations where hardship was claimed. The situation was somewhat relieved in 1980 by limiting the deduction for arrears to £1.20 per week. Where the debt amounts to two or three thousand pounds this provision looks like a lifetime of deductions ahead. In order not to put a premium on non-payment, one has to remember in fairness the person next door who, with the same income and circumstances, never gets into debt.

Under normal circumstances such a situation would not arise. The housing manager would call regularly for the rent; the Northern Ireland Electricity Board representative would call and advise the purchase of weekly stamps to spread the debt—in certain circumstances the supply would be cut off. The gas man emptied the coin meters regularly. However, a Supplementary Benefits visitor had been shot; in February 1976 an electricity meter reader had both his legs blown off when he set off a booby trap, intended for the army, in an unoccupied house; gas meter men had been frequently robbed. Thus the Northern Ireland Electricity Board did not order any staff to go and cut off electricity supplies, gas meters were broken open regularly and one heard of the near farcical situation of users being asked to empty their meters and bring in the money! Where there was very infrequent meter reading there was usually someone on hand who would alter the wiring to bypass the meter and so provide free electricity.

By the end of the decade the situation had improved and statutory workers felt more free to move around except at times of high emotion, such as the death of the first hunger striker. Other supply service workers felt themselves very vulnerable to intimidation. In a situation where one's background could quickly be checked, workers had to be chosen carefully for repair jobs to telephones, electric cables, sewerage and water supplies. Sometimes they just were not available and the service organisations were also loath to send in valuable mobile equipment if it was liable to be damaged or stolen. The house building programme has also, at times, been held up.

On the whole it has been easier for nursing and social workers to carry on with their job and to go all over Belfast. It is usual to man local offices with staff of matching denominations to the area concerned but not exclusively so. In ghetto areas where the grapevine is active, the outsider is regarded with suspicion. On one occasion the Belfast Voluntary Welfare Society was advised to withdraw one of its students (on a field work placement) from the Ballymurphy area. Seconded from a statutory office and on a professional social studies course, he was a mature student conventionally dressed. It was being said in Ballymurphy that he was spying for the army! This Society's social workers went to clients' homes in every part of Belfast, as did its domiciliary laundry service for incontinent people. The van was never interfered with. The van attached to Voluntary Service Belfast (VSB), used for collecting secondhand furniture from donors and delivering to families in need, was hijacked in the early days in the Turf Lodge area. It was handed back when the young volunteer driver was recognised as a member of a local Belfast pop group.

So many buses have been hijacked, used as barricades or burnt that during bad times of rioting they are withdrawn from some routes. In 1971 the city bus service was first withdrawn from the Falls Road and some enterprising individuals purchased secondhand London taxis and ran them on the bus routes. By filling the taxis and charging the same fare as the buses they became a profitable venture. At first some ran illegally, unlicensed and not passed for carrying the public. When the police caught up with the situation all was put in order and in some areas of Belfast the 'black taxis' have become a feature of city life. They are to be seen also on the Protestant Shankill Road. It was said that the taxi owners at times encouraged youths to hijack and burn buses as it was good for trade.

Squatting, though now under better control, has been a very real problem for many and in particular the body in charge of statutory housing, the Northern Ireland Housing Executive. The practice became a problem in 1969 when after the house burnings some 500 homes were required. Due to intimidation and fear, other houses were made vacant as families moved to a safer area and became potential squatters themselves. People had to be housed anyhow, and the state was loath to turn families out—when they had no ready places to put them. There was a tendency to legitimise some of the moves, by eventually giving the occupier a rent book. To some extent such people jumped the queue and meant that the legitimate applicant had to wait longer for a house.

Some people have turned to the paramilitary organisations, particularly on the Protestant side and asked them to put them into a house, claiming that they can get nothing from the Housing Executive. Because of such action it is necessary in certain areas to ensure that there is a simultaneous move—the new tenant moves in as the departing tenant leaves. The writer had the experience of supervising a change in tenancy in East Belfast, and seeing the new tenant quickly installed when 20 minutes later the UDA arrived with their tenant. There were in Northern Ireland about 2,000 units squatting in 1972 and by 1973 this figure had reached about 5,000. It remained at this figure for some time and is slowly diminishing.

Community relations

At the end of 1969 a Ministry of Community Relations was formed, together with an independent Community Relations Commission. The object in theory was to make a positive attempt at improving relations between the two communities. The Ministry, however, was very small and was not able to carry much weight at Stormont Cabinet level. Its chief function became that of providing grants under a Social Needs Act, for building and equipping community centres in deprived, and therefore often riot-torn, areas.

The Commission had a dual role, that of promoting good relations in the field and of advising the Government on possible action. Their first Chairman, who was a Catholic, Dr. Maurice Hayes, resigned in 1972 because none of his Commission's recommendations were acted upon. The Commission did good work in grant aiding some reconciling organisations, and bringing groups together to discuss vital issues. It published a constructive and well produced quarterly, 'Community Forum', and it was along these lines of community development, rather than community relations across the divide that the Commission made its main impact. This was an easier field in which to work, but was also due to the fact that the first Director, Hywel Griffiths, was trained and skilled in this line. At its peak the Commission had a team of 16 community development officers promoting and assisting community groups throughout Ulster. In its report published in 1973 it was noted that 394 such groups were receiving support.

When the 1973 Assembly was operative and the Power-Sharing Executive set up, Ivan Cooper was given the post as Minister for Community Relations. He felt that there was no need for a Commission since the Executive itself represented community relations in action. He wanted community groups to look to and support the Assembly. He was not to know that the Executive was shortly to fall, but the move was unfortunately too precipitate, because in succeeding years the advice of a broadly based independent group advising the Secretary of State would have been no bad thing, especially if it were a two-way exercise with the Northern Ireland Office requesting such a commission to comment confidentially on possible action. The Westminster Minister in charge of the Community Relations Department, Lord Donaldson, did hesitate about reviving the Commission, but decided against it and eventually phased out the Department also. The grant aiding functions were shared by the Departments of Education and Health and Social Services, to whom many of the Commission's field officers were transferred. The making of grants was then passed to the 26 District Councils, advised by their community service sections. Since 1980 financial strictures have required a new element of cost effectiveness to be proved by the recipients.

Community associations

The rapid growth of these community associations represents another phenomenon of the years of violence. This mirrored a similar development in Great Britain but in Northern Ireland it has been both more extensive and to some extent more radical.

Prior to 1968 paternalism was dying out more slowly than in Great Britain. In the Catholic community the Church still claimed the strong allegiance of so many. Those needing help looked to the members of the Conferences of St. Vincent de Paul. The Credit Union, a thrift society, not necessarily a Catholic organisation, but largely supported by and used by Catholics in Northern Ireland, was parish based but drew on professional help. Protestants, as well as looking to their churches, relied on the Orange Order and their Unionist representatives. Help and aid came from societies based outside the ghetto areas.

There were a few locally run old people's clubs and some pensioners' associations. Tenants' associations came and went from time to time, and were in the main protest organisations formed to fight some specific rent increase or to agitate for some amenity in the area. The Ballymurphy Tenants' Association was an early pioneer in the sphere of community association. Their members had had some vision of their future role and had raised funds and commenced building a community centre before violence broke out.

Following the violence and increased segregation in 1969, people living in these ghetto and housing estates around the perimeter of Belfast and provincial towns felt an increased spirit of togetherness. In Catholic areas there was the feeling that the police had let them down and were not acceptable. It was their fellow members who had come to their aid rather than the Belfast City Welfare after the riots and it was to their own relief agencies that members looked—the Central Citizens' Defence Committee has been mentioned. The fact also that people did not move about in the city so much, particularly at night, added to this community feeling and the need to have a local community association.

Particularly in the Catholic estates in Londonderry, the Bogside and the Creggan, there was a new found sense of self-realisation. Under the guidance mainly of John Hume and Ivan Cooper the inhabitants had been encouraged to break out from their apathetic hopelessness and to think and act for themselves. The Civil Rights marches had in October 1968 led to a package deal of reforms. They had given a lead and thanks to the insistence of the leaders, it had been non-violent. A former teacher and later community worker in Londonderry has written: 'In 1968 there was abroad a wonderful feeling that change was not only desirable but possible, and that we were on the brink of a new era of enlightenment and understanding.'[13] The community association in the Bogside was an early example of this attitude.

In Belfast there was a local demand that the houses completely burnt in 1969, particularly in Bombay Street, should be re-built. The City Corporation had planned no move, but under pressure they produced some existing plans and commenced re-building. Again there was a local outcry; the proposed houses would not suit the large families in the area. With private finance and the designs of the architect who had designed the Ballymurphy Tenants' Community Centre, a whole new street was built.

This could not quite be called 'self-help' since professional help and expertise came from outside the area. In general the Catholic communities were more closely integrated and help more forthcoming from lawyers, doctors, architects and business people on the Catholic side than on the Protestant side. Here in the workers' areas people had broken with their leaders, who it was felt had let them down and given way to what was seen as the pro-Catholic British Labour Party (then in office) and to the pro-Catholic army on the streets.

The proroguing of the Stormont Government in 1972 served to increase reliance on local area leaders and when the local authorities gave way in 1973 to District Councils with truncated powers the split was complete. On both sides of the religious divide local voluntary leaders came to the fore in many areas. They were people dedicated to the task of serving the community in which they lived, and what they lacked in administrative expertise they made up for in hard work and they learned quickly.

Two trends then became discernible. One was the introduction of more professional expertise, firstly from the Commission's field officers and later, when the community associations were given grant aid to employ their own organisers, these were often people who had received some training. Secondly the very existence of this grant aid and the need to report to the statutory body almost inevitably carried with it some supervision of policy. The former amateur leaders therefore no longer had the same independence, nor commanded the same support from the communities concerned and those who looked upon the community organisations as the birth of a new political order were disappointed.

So indeed had those who saw in the community movement the way to reconciliation. For one thing, each community, in finding a new group awareness, was concerned with its own area. It is true that the various associations did come together across the divide in the 'Community Organisations of Northern Ireland' (CONI). It is true also that the representatives found that they all frequently faced the same problems and had much in common, but the emotive bonds which cause the old divisions were stronger than those which provide for community group loyalty. In East Belfast there was in existence at the time of the formation of CONI, an Ulster Community Action Group, uniting Loyalist community groups. The real power, however, was held by the UDA. In West Belfast an emotional event like the death of the first hunger striker led to an upsurge of Provisional IRA sympathy, which weakened the influence of community groups in the area and allowed the Republicans to gain more power.

In 1980 the Community Education Forum lists an Index of 600 Community Groups in the Province and this does not include locally based sports or games clubs. The way has now been opened for local ability and potential leadership where before it had only come to the surface through the exceptional person. The person with the good brain gets 'A' levels and goes to the University. He or she tends to leave the area. Local leadership is another thing. To aid community development there are community resource centres, co-operative printing workshops, some community education schemes and in Belfast an Open College, independently run, which arranges courses in subjects and crafts for which there is a demand. The aim of this type of folk high school is to cater for those with a genuine interest in the subject, and not with the object of passing examinations.

Violence and youth

Much has been written on the subject of violence and its effect on the children of Northern Ireland. It became a common sight on television to see youths stoning the police or army. Press photographs were shown of children acting out the deeds of their elders—some regretfully acted out to satisfy the requirements of the media, but, alas, all too frequently present in reality.

The general relaxation of the strict bonds of parents and of society, which gave young people a new freedom in western society in the fifties and sixties, affected Northern Ireland also, though with a certain time lag. There was more money about, travel and movement were easier, alcohol and drugs more available than for previous generations, sexual permissiveness increased. These, with an earlier reaching of maturity and with social security available from the age of 16, were present in Northern Irish society to some degree. It might have been expected that with this revolt against the standards of their parents that youth in Northern Ireland would have made a break with the old sectarian traditions. This did not happen; whatever young folk may have thought about parental control they faithfully accepted all the ancient tribal shibboleths and translated them into gang warfare.

A playgroup organiser in Belfast wrote, 'to see themselves on television, to know that they are making world headlines, to feel themselves shaping history, to sing songs that immortalise their names'[15] is heady wine and, given some part by their elders in a violent action, command for them great respect from their playgroup.

On the Catholic side the action started with stoning the army and the

RUC and then throwing home-made petrol bombs. The army literally drew their fire and from these youngsters the leaders of the Provisionals gathered recruits for more lethal tasks. Young Protestants seeing this notoriety formed their own gangs, such as the Tartan gangs of East Belfast. They beat up young Catholics, and in turn these gangs became a recruiting ground for Loyalist paramilitary organisations. These youths were soon to find themselves before the courts. As was seen in the last chapter, from the study made by Messrs Boyle, Hadden and Hillyard the Republicans tended to be younger than the Loyalists and less likely to have convictions. The authors explain that Loyalists who wish to take up the fight against the IRA have the alternatives of joining a legitimate organisation, like the Ulster Defence Regiment or the RUC. One cannot enter either organisation if one has a criminal record—so in such a case one turns to the UDA or some splinter group.

In 1979 the ages of those coming before the courts was on average higher on both sides than in 1975. The level of violence having subsided there was not the same urge for young Loyalists to take active part. On the Republican side, the organisation was becoming more sophisticated, secretive and cellular in pattern. In the eighties those living in the Republican areas were saying, 'There was a time when you knew who was a Provo; now you don't know who they are.' Presumably if any are caught and questioned their knowledge of the organisation is limited to few contacts.

The position in schools

Although horrific stories of teachers held at gun point by members of their class may be discounted, the problems of teaching classes containing junior members of paramilitary organisations can well be appreciated. The path of the teacher who tries to explain the evils of violence in such a situation cannot be an easy one to tread.

Again it must be stressed that it depends where the school is situated. There are secondary schools (i.e. secondary modern in GB) in non-violent areas where life continues almost oblivious of the political situation. This would apply certainly to most of the 78 grammar schools in the Province. The Minister of State for Education, Lord Peter Melchett (1976–9), was anxious to bring in comprehensive schools, but this was firmly resisted by the grammar schools. His Tory successor, Lord Elton, did not make any move in this direction. In the Catholic grammar schools the pupils will tend to have closer involvement with the politics of the local situation, and to have more carefully documented arguments to support their case than in non-Catholic schools, due, for one thing, to learning Irish history as opposed to the British-based history which is taught in non-Catholic schools. Otherwise they both share many of the same examination worries and interests in a society which opens for school pupils opportunities in sporting events, music and the arts and above all travel unknown to previous generations.

There are still not a great number of occasions when those of school age meet across the religious divide. It is almost nil at the primary school age where the schools serve the ghettos or housing estates. Otherwise there are opportunities to meet on conference occasions, for instance, those school conferences organised by UNESCO or the Council for Education in World Citizenship. There have been some pupil-based organisations between Protestant and Catholic schools. On one occasion school staffs were worried, not because of the Catholic-Protestant links, but because the group was 'left' in politics and said to be manipulated by an outside organisation. As the school population is constantly changing, it is difficult to provide continuity in any pupil-inspired organisation.

In the eighties the need for new teachers has decreased and with two Catholic teacher training colleges, St. Mary's for women and St. Joseph's for men, and one large non-Catholic one, Stranmillis, the need for places is considerably over-provided. In 1974 there were 2,000 new student teachers enrolled; in 1980, 620. All attempts to bring the three together and so effect appreciable saving has failed as the Catholic institutions feel they have a special duty to train teachers in their own spiritual tradition.[16]

There has always been meeting and good co-operation at the universities and the Polytechnic. In 1960 the proportion of Catholic students at Queen's University was 22%—something under expectancy per population figures—but in 1978–9 the figure was 43%. It is not clear whether some of this increase may not be due to a greater proportion of Protestant students seeking places in universities across the water.

Holidays for children

There have been many attempts to arrange shared holidays for children. As well as Corrymeela and the Harmony Community Trust, some organisations have been formed specifically for the arranging of holidays, for example, Holiday Projects West, based in Londonderry, and Discovery Holidays in Belfast. More recently a Northern Ireland Children's Holidays Scheme has been set up which sends mixed groups of children to a holiday home at Narin, Co. Donegal.

Many other organisations have arranged mixed holidays for children. Some united councils of churches in the UK and even overseas organisations have made great efforts and shown great generosity in bringing Northern Ireland children for a holiday. Obviously the children have a great time and gain something from the visit. In response to such kindness the Department of Education, for a period, made grants towards the cost of travel involved. Usually the children get on well together and local divisions are forgotten in the excitement of new surroundings with many activities laid on for their enjoyment. Once they return home, however, they are absorbed back into the sectarian home environment with all the old prejudices and fears. It is understood that the hosts wish to be involved with the children, but children will mix just as well nearer at home but away from the ghetto atmosphere at a much smaller cost. Funds saved could be used to bring them together again during term time, when it is very unlikely that they would otherwise meet.

Integrated education

Opinion polls carried out in 1967, 1968, 1972 and 1973 by the *Sunday Times*, *Fortnight* and the Social Science Research Council all show that a large proportion of children and parents—Protestant and Catholic alike—would welcome shared schools. A movement was started during the seventies, All Children Together, to try to achieve some measure of integrated education to break the position where about 90% of Catholic children go to Catholic schools and 99.5% of Protestants go to non-Catholic schools.

A breakthrough was achieved when the Alliance Party peer, Lord Dunleath, promoted a Bill in the House of Lords in June 1977 to facilitate integrated education. This Bill was the brain child of Basil McIvor, a barrister who had been the Minister for Education in the Executive of the 1974 Assembly. The basis of the Bill was that if 75% of the parents of any state school requested that it should be a shared school, then the appropriate education authority had to carry out arrangements to make this possible. Eventually the Bill passed both Houses and on 26 May 1978 it became law. No school so far has taken advantage of the Act—except from the parents of a primary school which was about to be closed down. The scheme is not aimed to do away with church schools but to create an alternative. The Catholic Church, however, remains very much against the scheme. Wishing to maintain good relations with the Catholic hierarchy, neither the Church of Ireland nor the Presbyterian Assembly has made any specific attempts to encourage initiatives to be taken under the Act, though earlier both denominations had passed resolutions in favour of integrated education.

All Children Together, disappointed at the lack of response, has gone ahead and opened a special shared school on the perimeter of Belfast which they have named Lagan College. The project has the backing of two large trusts, but will have to prove its educational viability over two years before the Department of Education will accept the school for the purpose of making the normal per capita grants. Fees must be charged and the early years will be difficult. It is one thing to wish the school well, another to send your children to an untried establishment. The progress of the school will be watched with great interest.

Youth unemployment

The problem of finding a meaningful occupation for school leavers is now as intractable as the sectarian issue. It has always been a greater problem in Northern Ireland than in Great Britain with more pressure therefore to develop schemes for industrial government training. There are now 13 Government Training Centres across the Province providing for 3,300 training places. These have to be shared with adults when trades have become redundant, and it would appear that the scheme is about to be expanded. A wide range of skills are covered, with emphasis on engineering and construction trades. Some firms help the programme by taking on young people for training and colleges of further education are endeavouring to supplement places available.

A job provision undertaking to include a certain amount of instruction was set up in 1973. Named Enterprise Ulster, it engages mainly in amenity improvement and environmental schemes and has a work force of around 1,800 young people.

A scheme similar to the Community Employment Programme was set up in Northern Ireland in 1981. Known as the Assisted Community Employment Scheme (ACE) it makes it possible for voluntary enterprises to take on staff which otherwise they could not afford. To gain government acceptance any project must show some community benefit and must not take the place of paid labour. A grant of 90% of salary (up to a stated ceiling) is available for an agreed number of employees who have been out of work for a year or more. The government will take on a scheme for two years, but each employee can only be grant-aided for one year.

Earlier in the chapter, the furniture service run by Voluntary Service Belfast was mentioned. Furniture collected from donors is stored in a central warehouse in the city awaiting requests for distribution. Through Manpower Services a skilled joiner has been provided to train young unemployed men and women to carry out repair work on furniture which comes in damaged. The scheme later developed to include upholstery work also. At the time of writing the work force consists of a manager, three tutors and about 30 trainees, in what is called a Work Preparation Unit, set up as a company separate from VSB. Of those trained, about 45% have been able to obtain jobs. Obviously such schemes cannot create permanent employment, but the Province needs a more highly-skilled work force to meet modern requirements of industry, and it demonstrates to school leavers that they can become skilled craftsmen.

Supplementary Benefits regulations now permit those signing on for work to give full-time voluntary help to church and other voluntary bodies, without loss of benefit. This makes it possible for those without work to do something useful. The volunteer must, naturally, take up paid work if it becomes available.

Welcome as schemes like ACE are in the present employment crisis, they can in no way compensate for the large loss of jobs due to closure and redundancy. The impact of not being wanted in the community is likely to have a greater long-term effect than all the violence that has occurred.

6 Voluntary reconciling organisations

It would be all too easy to dismiss the achievements of voluntary organisations in the field of reconciliation as being of no appreciable significance when measured against the continuing violence.

If after 12 or more years of civil unrest the community appears to be more polarised than ever it could be argued that those working through the various peace organisations might have been better employed helping the handicapped in our midst, or even digging their own gardens.

This would be a mistaken judgement, for so much of what has happened in the Province in the last 15 years shows a much greater degree of co-operation and understanding for which the reconciling organisations can claim some credit. The main enemy is the overt violence of the few for it evokes retaliatory violence from various factions as well as from those responsible for security. Violence increases fear and fuels tribal animosity, and the peace worker, if he or she is honestly facing up to the situation, must admit that the violent few have behind them, on both sides, a penumbra of tacit support from their tribes, an area where the reconciler has been able to make very little headway.

THE IRISH ASSOCIATION

The doyen of reconciling bodies, the Irish Association, was founded in 1938 by the late Major General Hugh Montgomery of Fivemile town in Co. Tyrone. He had been a former Minister of Education and leader of the Northern Ireland Senate and he became the first President of the Irish Association.

The aims of the Association were (and remain so today) to encourage respect for the convictions of others; to correct misrepresentation and to discourage intolerance and intimidation. Its members were drawn from the higher echelons of the socio-economic scale and its conferences and lectures were on the 'safe' subjects of archaeology, the arts and cultural and economic interests. Visits were paid to places of cultural interest. There are two governing committees, one in the North and one in the Republic. The reconciliation was therefore cross-border as well as cross-denominational, and it was probably for this reason regarded with suspicion by the Unionist Party. Gradually the Association became bolder and started looking at the more crucial differences between the Protestant and Catholic communities in Northern Ireland, a 'border line' its members thought more difficult to cross than the political one across the country. In 1959 to try to tackle these divisions a study of group relations was commissioned and the findings published in book form in 1962 by the Oxford University Press with the title *The Northern Ireland Problem*. The aim was to explain the situation as objectively as possible and to show how events looked when viewed from the opposing sides of the divide. It did not seek to apportion blame and whilst indicating avenues of hopeful action did not try to produce a blueprint solution.

To some the lack of judgement appeared a defect and a weakness but the basic aim was to open minds closed to all but their tribal shibboleths and not to turn them away by appearing biased. When the eyes of the world had been turned on the problems of Ireland following the civil disturbances, chapters were added to bring the book up to date and it was re-published as a paperback in 1972.

To date the Irish Association has discussed just about every facet of life in Ireland, and over the past 15 years it has published a number of monographs and booklets usually based on papers given to members. In 1971 a questionnaire on community relations was distributed on a broad basis. Some questions were open-ended and no quantitative analysis made as the survey could not have claimed to be a weighted analysis of the population as a whole.

Two annual awards are given, one for students—'an extended essay'—and the other for school and youth organisations, on various projects for promoting better understanding between those of different denominations or political affiliations.

The membership tends to remain somewhat static and there is no specific drive to expand or increase it.

THE CORRYMEELA COMMUNITY

In the early sixties Rev. Ray Davey, the Presbyterian Dean of Residence at Queen's University, felt that the Church in Ireland was so encased in its own pietism that it was neglecting the deeper Christian witness of reconciliation and love towards all men. In this he was backed by some of his students and other kindred spirits. They were inspired by the ideals of the Iona Community; they wanted to share in the searchings of the clerics in the Taizé Community in Burgundy towards the full meaning of Christian involvement. Above all they were encouraged by the visits to Belfast of Pastor Tullio Vinay, who had founded the village of love, Agape, in Italy.

They found that they were rebels, but within the Church and not against it, and their story is well told by Alf McCreary, an award winning journalist in a paperback *Corrymeela—the Search for Peace.*[1] He tells of an act of faith by Ray Davey and his supporters in purchasing a former Holiday Fellowship centre situated on a fine clifftop site, near Ballycastle. This chalet type building had around it room for expansion and a beautiful view across the sea to the bird sanctuary isle of Rathlin.

With the help of numerous volunteer workcamps (themselves a good way of developing a group spirit and of breaking down barriers) the house was ready for use at the end of October 1965. It was fitting that Pastor Vinay should come from Italy to perform the opening ceremony for this 'Hill of Harmony'—appropriately the meaning of Corrymeela.

The Province was soon to realise that there was a new centre at Ballycastle for the following Easter Corrymeela staged its first big conference. The organisers realised that the year 1966 was a year of challenge. It was 50 years since 1916, for the Nationalist the year of the Easter Rising in Dublin by Sinn Fein, 16 of whose leaders were to be executed as a result; for the Unionist the 50th anniversary of the Battle of the Somme, when Ulster regiments suffered great losses. As was noted in the first chapter it was a time of great opportunity also, and a number of leading speakers were invited to speak on the subject 'Community 1966'. Among these was the Prime Minister, Terence O'Neill, who saw in Corrymeela a place where the 'two traditions' could meet and learn to live together. His speech was well received by the press, but incurred Catholic hierarchical disapproval when he raised the divisive problem of whether separate church schools 'were not a barrier to the promotion of communal understanding'.

Corrymeela did not seek publicity of this kind. Its committee and supporters preferred to work quietly and practically, bringing differing groups together to learn to see each other's point of view as being genuinely held even when agreement could not always be found.

When the civil disturbances broke out, families harassed by rioting night after night, or living with intimidating threats, were invited to Corrymeela for a short break. In an atmosphere of peace and understanding they were able to return refreshed having experienced something of the continuing goodness in life through being with those who cared. Parents were particularly worried about their children and at times of great stress (such as the riots following the 1971 re-introduction of internment) groups of children were evacuated to Corrymeela. Often Protestant and Catholic children away from the divisive influence of their segregated ghetto homes were able to get on well enough together.

For this type of activity more accommodation was required and a 'village' extension was built with financial and physical help from groups inspired by the Corrymeela spirit. These groups had been formed in support of Corrymeela's work not only in Northern Ireland but in London and Coventry. There was a close affinity between what Corrymeela was doing and the type of link which had been forged between Coventry and Dresden (marked by the International Centre at Coventry). There was an exchange of volunteers offering service in these two cities which had suffered so terribly in the 1939–45 war. Corrymeela was invited to become one of Coventry's 'Cross of Nails' centres, and from Coventry came groups of workers, backed by funds, to clear a site and see a fine new building at Ballycastle—the Coventry House of Reconciliation. Other continental links were made and helpers come annually from Germany, Switzerland and elsewhere.

As well as being a holiday and conference centre for many types of reconciling and community groups, Corrymeela sponsors its own conferences. Difficult topics are tackled—policing in a violent setting, problems of drug addiction and alcoholism, and the ever-present problem of seeking a way out of the Province's violence morass.

A new venture took place over a week in July 1981—a 'Summerfest' on the meaning and relevance of the Lord's Prayer to the world today. Each day there were study groups led by a wide variety of well-informed experts and well-known speakers including Mother Teresa.

THE INTERNATIONAL PEACE AND AID ORGANISATIONS

The two devastating air raids on Belfast in the spring of 1941 must have provided the citizens (1,000 of whom were killed in two raids) with striking evidence that Ulster could be no longer 'a place apart' as far as the effects of modern warfare are concerned. Yet it has always been more difficult than in the rest of the UK to find support for the international peace movement. Even the Campaign for Nuclear Disarmament in its halcyon days of the late fifties called forth minimal support and the United Nations Association finds that events in New York and Geneva appear very remote. The 1980 resurgence of CND is meeting with an encouraging response from younger folk and as with the earlier campaign it provides a useful occasion for Protestant and Catholic to work together on a common cause, without having to be continually conscious of the local divisions.

For the most part, the drift towards war in the thirties and the emergence of the H-bomb in the fifties, made the local differences appear to members of the Peace Pledge Union and the Fellowship of Reconciliation as petty family squabbles by comparison. However, with the commencement of the IRA campaign (1956–62) aimed at installations along the border, the FoR felt that some effort should be made to face divisions at home. In conjunction with the Irish Pacifist Movement in Dublin (the Irish Section of the War Resisters' International) annual conferences were held in Drogheda, Dublin and Belfast which brought Protestant and Catholic from the North and from the South together. Ironically it was more difficult then to find people willing to cross this sectarian and national divide than it was 20 years later after violence had re-segregated the bulk of the population in the North.

The 1958 conference had a familiar ring. A solicitor in the Sinn Fein Party argued the case that 'the British troops must go'. A member of FoR, William Boyd, who represented the Northern Ireland Labour Party at Stormont, spoke in favour of maintaining the British link within which framework he proposed various reforms. The 'troops'—four Irish regiments often abroad and never seen on the streets—were felt by Protestant workers to serve as a final line of defence should Sinn Fein take action.

In subsequent years various divisive topics—Church and State, mixed marriages, education, capital punishment and civil rights and responsibilities—were openly tackled.

The Fellowship pioneered work camps in Londonderry in 1969 bringing a score of volunteers from the UK and Europe to help at a Catholic orphanage. They lived in a parochial hall in the heart of the Bogside area and organised a play scheme for the many children who flocked around the hall to find out what was happening. The volunteers made many friends in the area and some returned at Christmas to stay with one or two of these families. By this time there had been violence in this area and these were valuable contacts which were maintained when FoR returned during the following summer and lived then in the Protestant Waterside district.

In 1972 other groups had come to work in Londonderry and so FoR started similar summer playgroups in Lurgan in 1973. Lurgan, a town of some 25,000 inhabitants is 25 miles from Belfast and is roughly half Protestant and half Catholic. Although not noted for bad disturbances, as in situations where there is a type of 50/50 division, there is considerable tension. The volunteers have always operated in both a Catholic and a Protestant housing estate, but it took about four years of summer activities before the children began to mix in their home town. The ideal is to get the parents running joint playgroups during all school holidays. That has not been achieved but some of the children have been brought together during the year at a cottage, near Belfast, run by the Quaker Service Committee.

Pax Christi also have been running play schemes since 1976 in the neighbouring town of Portadown. As the schemes coincide the volunteers meet and compare notes. These schemes have been run from the UK Pax Christi office, but there is now a small Pax Christi group in Northern Ireland. There is also a small branch of the Père Pire movement, a third world and refugee aid body founded by the eponymous Nobel Peace Prize laureate the late Dominique Pire. This body runs a 'University of Peace' at Huy outside Brussels and some people from Northern Ireland, Protestant as well as Catholic, have attended their short courses.

A contribution from the Northern Ireland FoR was the founding in 1961 of a branch of the War on Want movement. This was an attempt to acknowledge the indivisible nature of peacemaking when the needs of the third world were not so universally accepted as they have become 20 years later. In the present context the salient issue is that the inaugural War on Want launching meeting was addressed by both a Protestant and a Catholic, and this active branch has remained a shared effort, running successful secondhand shops in a number of towns in the Province.

From 1962 to 1965 the Freedom from Hunger Campaign drew help from the existing third world fund-raising bodies to support what turned out to be a very successful irrigation and rice growing project near the foot of Mount Kenya. Thirty-six committees were formed throughout the Province; some were initiated by Catholics, some by Protestants, and in all cases the final result was a joint one. Sponsoring meetings were usually held in the town council chambers—in some towns the first time a fully shared co-operative project had ever taken place. In the final report at the closing down of the Campaign, it was pointed out that the target had been safely achieved. 'Those who have worked so hard, who have given so generously, would not want thanks; all of us have been in this grand endeavour together, and because we realised the immensity of the need, we forgot our own sectarian differences and worked in harmony together. In so doing, we were ourselves enriched.'

Mention has been made of Pierre Ceresole as the founder of the work camp movement. This was the Service Civil International, and the British branch of the International Voluntary Service first came to Northern Ireland in 1955 when parties worked at Childhaven, a Methodist orphanage and holiday home, and also at a Rudolf Steiner school for mentally handicapped children at Glencraig House overlooking Belfast Lough. This was a study/work project and the volunteers looked at areas of religious tension. Parties have continued to come to Northern Ireland since this date and there is now a local IVS office in Belfast with a full-time organiser. There has always been across the board support at home and members of both communities have shared in IVS work abroad.

The contribution of the Society of Friends in Northern Ireland to the reconciliation scene has been channelled mainly through the Peace and Service Committees. In 1969 and 1971 Friends become involved with the needs of those acutely affected by the Belfast riots. Both meeting houses in the city were used as emergency refuges for families engulfed by mob riots.

In 1972 it was Friends who were able to respond to the need of visitors to the internment camp at Long Kesh by providing a simple canteen at the gate of the prison. As the internment camp expanded and became a large modern prison, so Friends' facilities developed with the addition of a playgroup, and counselling and transport services. Their Service Committee in its concern for human need has developed projects including work with unemployed youth and help for the mentally confused. In 1981 a cottage centre was set up to give children disturbed by the violence a number of constructive activities.

THE HARMONY COMMUNITY TRUST

For some time the Northern Ireland branch of IVS had been contemplating the purchase of a house in the country where children from the ghetto areas could come together and experience a completely new type of life together. The obtaining of funds appeared an insuperable problem until Belfast Rotary Club were fired by the idea. With their customary generosity and flair for fund-raising their members raised £30,000 and in April 1975 formed, with IVS, the Harmony Community Trust. The type of country house with extensive grounds required came on the market and in July 1975 Glebe House, Kildief, Co. Down, was purchased for £40,000.

Since that time children from the city areas in Ulster have come to spend usually a ten-day period, Catholics and Protestants together, to work on the farmland and to play and get to know their opposite numbers.

To help the two co-ordinators, long-term and short-term volunteers come to give service. Young people come from many different countries for an annual international work camp which preserves the IVS link and which enables extra constructional work to be undertaken. The success of Glebe House owes so much to the original co-ordinator, Helen Honeyman, who came to Belfast first in 1970 as the leader of an IVS playgroup which was part of the summer play schemes programme of Voluntary Service Belfast.

The children who come to Glebe House work on the farm and with chickens, ducks and goats and more recently, a cow. There are beaches nearby and they have opportunities for horse-riding and camping trips to the Mournes are planned. For cold or wet weather there are various craft activities which have been developed and added to year by year. A kiln has now been donated and the children's efforts at pottery can now be fired.

The Department of Education in 1979 approved a 75% grant aid for house improvements costing £30,000. Fund raising is still a major priority for the voluntary proportion of the capital cost and for the general running also as the Department of Education's running cost grant does not cover expenses.

THE VOLUNTARY ORGANISATIONS AND THE POLITICAL SCENE

As has been seen 1968 was a turning point in Northern Ireland's history. It was the last occasion when overdue reforms might have been placed on the statute book without any violence and with a healing effect. It was also International Human Rights Year. For over a year the Belfast United Nations Association had been planning some action to mark the year in Northern Ireland. A broadly-based committee was appointed and the year was launched by an ecumenical inaugural service, in the main hall of Queen's University, quite an event in itself at the time (December 1967). Under the patronage of the Governor of Northern Ireland the committee got to work and with the help of specialist legal advice sent a carefully argued memorandum to the Stormont Government recommending the repeal of the Special Powers Act. This Act, which the Nationalist minority felt was directed against them, was seen by the committee as the chief breach in Northern Ireland of the International Declaration of Human Rights. It was argued that there was on the statute book, following the 1926 General Strike, Emergency Powers legislation which would give the State all the power required to deal with any emergency.

Emanating mainly from some members of the tiny Liberal Party was the concept of a New Ulster Movement. The political parties were trapped by history and took intransigent stands along divisive lines: a new Ulster had to emerge, it was argued, in which the two traditions could combine to give a peaceful and a richer society.

By the time enough support had been gathered to enable a public meeting to be held it was February 1969 and events had overtaken the organisers. The emergent New Ulster Movement found itself obliged as a matter of some urgency to give support to all candidates who were in favour of Prime Minister O'Neill's reforms at the forthcoming elections. This was too narrow a political image for the New Ulster Movement but the situation did help towards a rapid expansion of membership which was to grow to over 5,000. Some local groups were formed in every constituency but the central committee set its face against becoming a political party. The majority of the early membership was drawn from those who, to Ulster's detriment, had had nothing to do with party politics. Both Protestants and Catholics of moderate views saw politics as an arid and bigoted arena in which they did not wish to soil their hands. The events of 1968 alerted them to the need to come forward and be counted. Those who felt strongest that the New Ulster Movement should be their new political party left and concentrated their energies in the Alliance Party which was formed a year later in April 1971.

Meanwhile NUM saw its role as an ideas organisation, acting both as a catalyst to encourage constructive action and also as a political pressure group. Under the guidance of their chairman, Brian Walker, an able team of workers got down to talking with representatives of a very wide spectrum of opinion in Northern Ireland, in Great Britain and in the Republic of Ireland, a spectrum which included illegal groups using violence as their policy.

NUM maintained an opposition to the Special Powers Act and engaged an international lawyer of repute, Dr. Maurice Bathurst, to state his opinion on the legality of the Irish border. The findings in favour of legality were never challenged, and this gave NUM the right base from which to urge 'the rule of law'.[2]

A series of booklets then followed over the next two years, including *The Reform of Stormont*, a commentary on the reforms already agreed to. NUM urged that Westminster must make it clear that the constitutional position of Northern Ireland was their responsibility and was inviolable. Stormont should then concentrate on the economic and social and particular regional needs within the Province and, provided they rejected all violence, work with minority parties—in other words what came to be known as power-sharing. NUM lobbied strongly for this idea with the Westminster Government and began to press for the proroguing of Stormont. The SDLP took the concept of power-sharing and made it central to their policy.

The re-introduction of internment without trial in August 1971 was strenuously opposed and with the consequent increase in violence the NUM Committee began to despair of Stormont itself being willing to make the necessary changes. Without abandoning their belief in devolution as the right long-term solution, NUM in November 1971 published another booklet, *The Way Forward*, calling upon Westminster to take charge, suspend Stormont temporarily and put in its place a 'commission' to run the Province.

A period of three years was suggested when it was hoped that a body of nominated administrators would have been able to demonstrate that power-sharing was realistic and effective and would be seen in no way to weaken the link with Great Britain.

When Stormont was in fact prorogued in March 1972 NUM pleaded with Catholic leaders and groups to come forward and seize this occasion to escape from their own 'siege mentality' and denounce unequivocally the continuing violent policy of the Provisional IRA. They made a special plea to Church leaders—both Protestant and Catholic—in this respect. Unfortunately it fell largely on deaf ears.

NUM sponsored some direct action also. In October 1971 a 'petition for sanity' drew some 20,000 signatures from all sections of the community. The petition called for an ending of all violence and the signatories pledged themselves to work for reconciliation and for a peaceable solution. NUM then invited a number of reconciliation organisations to publicise by vigils in Belfast the idea of a large Peace Rally. Some eight to ten thousand people did gather in the Botanic Park and quietly dedicated themselves to work for the ending of violence. For once an encouraging news item from Northern Ireland ousted the usual reports of violence on national television. Smaller rallies were organised in different parts of the Province—Newry, Armagh, Londonderry and elsewhere.

In April 1972 NUM invited others from other parties to join them in a 24 hours vigil for peace outside the offices of both the Official and the Provisional Sinn Fein in Dublin. It was left to the oft-divided 'moderates' to challenge the men of violence in this way. Loyalist groups were conspicuous by their absence, but the following weekend a protest march through Dublin was organised by citizens of the Republic as a direct follow-up to the NUM protest.

When the Sunningdale Agreement for the Power-Sharing Executive was announced NUM made two representations to an all-party committee in Dublin to undertake the need to drop their insistence on a Council of Ireland. Press comments had already appeared in Dublin euphoric over this move which they felt would open the door eventually to Irish unity. NUM saw that such statements would set the face of hard-line Unionism even further against any idea of power-sharing.

In 1975 after the fall of the Power-Sharing Executive and the re-establishment of Direct Rule, the Westminster Government proposed a Constitutional Convention where 78 elected delegates were asked to hammer out a workable solution for devolved rule. NUM pressed all delegates to do just this and not to rest on predetermined party manifestos from which they would not move.

By this time there were changes in the NUM Committee and some internal differences over policy. The Alliance Party had grown in strength and to a large extent was fulfilling the role of NUM. The steam had gone out of the movement but before finally closing down in the late seventies one more booklet of value was issued. A careful study was made of the possibilities of Northern Ireland operating as an independent unit, concluding that this was not a viable solution.

It is impossible to evaluate the influence or effect of NUM on public opinion but there is reason to believe that its publications and deputations did have some influence on decisions at Westminster. That the Assembly and Power-Sharing Executive did not endure in 1974 was Ulster's tragedy and not NUM's mistaken conception. One cannot usually resurrect a movement so closely bound up with an epoch of history, as was NUM with the first half of the decade of violence. The original concept of a New Ulster along shared lines is a necessity in the eighties as it was in 1968.

PROTESTANT AND CATHOLIC ENCOUNTER MOVEMENT (PACE)

Even if not living in a segregated ghetto in Belfast, or a provincial town, Northern Ireland citizens have always followed a segregated social and cultural life, meeting only in certain spheres of life—the fine arts, professional connections, etc. Church affiliation, stronger than in Great Britain and most European countries, has tended to increase this separateness.

The more active the congregation the greater the inducement to support church activities—joining the Christian Endeavour, the Mothers' Union, the men's fireside discussion group, the indoor bowls group—and for younger members the tennis and badminton club, the team in the churches' football league—and if the church was not excessively pietist, the drama group. The Catholic Church can match these with saints' days and novenas which require attendance.

To the Ulster ear it would not sound strange to hear—'Ach, you know big Jimmy McCleery, who lives up the hill and goes to the Reverend Greers' church'—as a means of identification. The influence of the affluent society, travel, TV and the motor car are steadily making inroads into this pattern, but even if one has no church affiliation one probably still knows to which church one is not affiliated!

Any Protestant denominational differences are minimal compared to the gulf between them and the Roman Catholic Church. In rural areas prior to the recent disturbances there was a happy enough modus vivendi. There were certain unwritten rules adhered to—no one proselytised across the main divide for example—and indeed one hears stories of the same men changing uniforms and playing in the local bands for the 12 July and 15 August rival tribal marches because of the shortage of local musicians.

The unwritten rules did not allow any co-operation to go too far. There must be no attending of each others' services, and one had to be careful not to sell land to the other side, or give them your trade. Ecumenism means to a Protestant a take-over by the vast monolithic Roman Catholic Church and in the pre-Vatican Council days Catholics often discouraged mixing which might lead to mixed marriages and a temptation to their flock to stray from the straight and narrow—the teaching of the true Church.

To the Reverend Desmond Mock, an English Presbyterian minister, such practices were a legacy from a previous age and did not belong to the twentieth century. He was also fearful of a violent Protestant response to the Civil Rights marches which were being spoken of in the summer of 1968. He wrote to the press suggesting that inter-denominational groups should meet regularly for discussion and prayer. He met with those who had responded favourably to his letter and after considerable discussion it was agreed that groups should be set up, if possible right across the Province, shared by Catholics and Protestants who would try to bring people together of different denominations to get to know each other, to learn to work together and to try to stop violence from breaking out.

It was agreed to call the movement Protestant and Catholic Encounter, the acronym of which conveniently spells PACE. Each group would have a Protestant and a Catholic chairman and the Committee would be balanced 50/50. PACE was formally launched in March 1969 with 30 founding members and a conference on 'Understanding each other' was held in Belfast. A visit was paid to the Prime Minister, Terence O'Neill, when it was recommended that there should be an official body run on the lines of PACE. A paper by a member of the Law Faculty at Queen's University was produced for governmental discussion. It was thought that this action had some influence on the Government's decision made during the summer to give consideration to a 'community relations' structure which materialised at the end of the year in the formation of a Ministry of Community Relations and an independent Community Relations Commission.

PACE continued to hold conferences in Belfast, and to gain in numbers and support. A branch was first set up at Ballymoney and then at Holywood, Dunmurry and in and around Belfast. The emphasis was placed on getting to know the person who belonged to the other tribe, and finding out what made him tick.

It was frequently found by members of both main groups that long accepted beliefs about the other 'side' were incorrect. In some towns the practice was followed of going round all the different denominations, attending the service and then meeting with the church members to hear about their history and tenets of their faith. It was usually found that the Protestant denominations held incorrect views of each other also. Once friendly contact was established then it was the time to tackle the difficult divisive questions—education, divorce, birth control, national identity—things which nice folk pushed under the carpet when they did not want to accentuate the divisions. At times one opened one's cupboard to display the skeletons.

When an operational grant had been obtained from the Community Relations Commission, a field officer was engaged. This was someone with time, patience, tact and tenacity, willing to go round provincial towns seeking out those who would attend an inaugural meeting and form a local branch.

The movement saw that once a branch has found its feet and is secure the emphasis shifts from 'encounter' to enterprise and endeavour. Groups start thinking of things to do together and functions have been arranged to make money for numerous charities and third world organisations. Joint carol and prayer services have been held, two towns have formed branches of Citizens' Advice Bureaux, another a War on Want shop, and two areas have produced a booklet on the amenities of the town. Numerous holidays for children and the elderly have been arranged profiting on occasions from the generosity of groups of churches and other bodies in England or Scotland. In fact, this amounts to showing how projects of local significance should be jointly run throughout the Province.

At its peak, around 1975, PACE had 35 branches and a membership of about 2,000. Members receive a journal three times a year which is sent also to political and church leaders.

It has been difficult to retain vitality in some of the groups, particularly in towns where Protestants or Catholics have an overwhelming majority and where in consequence there is not the same tension as in the more equally divided areas.

In other towns similar groups have grown up. For instance, in Dungannon there was for a while an active organisation called FAN (Friends and Neighbours). In a divided area of Belfast a small group has kept together across the divide called the Duncairn Friendship Association. In Londonderry there is a Derry Peace and Reconciliation Centre. To push into these areas could be counterproductive.

By the late seventies the active PACE groups had dropped to between 15 and 20 but the increased tensions of the early eighties appear to be re-stimulating activity.

Detractors of PACE claim that the movement merely forms a pleasant club for liberal professionals who would meet in any case. The PACE Committee replies that numerous members have stated that before they came into the movement they had no friends across the divide and that in times of tension it requires no mean effort to stop even the liberals from slipping into a state of mental segregation. It is hard to get those who are more entrenched in tribal beliefs to 'encounter' each other. The fact that PACE is fairly well-known means it is something to be avoided by those with strongest views. Republicans and Loyalists no doubt regard it as ineffective, but dangerous if it became too strong, Republicans regarding it as a pro-establishment body and Loyalists as a pro-Catholic body tending to weaken Protestant resolve. However, even in a time of curtailment of grants the Department of Education is sufficiently satisfied to maintain its annual grant towards the running of this organisation.

FELLOWSHIP OF PRAYER FOR CHRISTIAN UNITY

An organisation which in many ways parallels PACE but one with much greater emphasis on prayer is the Fellowship of Prayer for Christian Unity. It was formed in 1968, the year of awakening, by members of the Church of Ireland, Methodist, Presbyterian, Catholic and Society of Friends denominations, who were concerned to stress the unity of all believers with particular emphasis on the value and power of prayer. Members were sought, the only condition for acceptance being that they would each pray daily that the unity for which Christ prayed might come about.

The first public event was planned for the week of Christian Unity in January 1969, when a hall was kept opened for prayer in a Catholic hall in Bank Street, Belfast. At the end of the week 214 new members had been added to the original sponsors. The Fellowship now numbers about 600. Some of these live in towns and country districts where joint prayer services are not easy to arrange but they are told of the events arranged and asked to support these in prayer.

Services are held in churches and halls and clergy of most denominations take part. During the Unity Week of Prayer an annual united church service is held in Belfast in a church of a different denomination each year.

Talks are also arranged for instance on attitudes to the Eucharist, the common Christian heritage and other subjects of a devotional nature.

WOMEN TOGETHER

Every new idea must start in someone's mind. Initiatives for reconciliation have taken root where the person with the vision goes courageously ahead and does something about it.

Mrs Ruth Agnew had been a cleaner in the Belfast Gas Works. She was distressed that her Catholic neighbours had left the area through fear and had moved to Catholic housing estates. She was worried that young boys still at school were tempted and pressurised into taking part in rioting and violent action. It was time, she felt, for mothers and for women in general to act. She was put in touch with a member of the PACE Committee, Mrs Monica Patterson, an English Catholic, who invited Ruth Agnew to a PACE Conference to be held in the Stranmillis Teacher Training College. There Ruth Agnew spoke from the floor saying that what was needed was not discussions in a college, but to get the women together in her street, women who lived in riot areas and knew at first hand what violence meant.

PACE members were delighted. Here was the possibility of a break-through at grass roots level, something that had seemed so difficult to achieve. Ruth Agnew was promised PACE's help and Monica Patterson gave up more and more of her time getting this women's movement off the ground, one which was to be known as 'Women Together'. She became their first chairman.

The first group meeting of Women Together took place in East Belfast in October 1970. Other groups followed in South Belfast and in the Ardoyne area of the city. Where due to segregated living conditions it was not geographically easy to mix Protestants and Catholics, they carried on in separate groups meeting together wherever possible.

Some women from the Protestant Shankill had befriended Catholics burnt out of their homes in and around Bombay Street in the first real outburst of violence in August 1969. These women formed the basis of another Women Together branch and brought with them a former Trade Union organiser, Sadie Patterson, who was to give them leadership when Monica Patterson (no relation) resigned and returned to live in England.

By 1977 there were seven groups of Women Together in Belfast and another two in the neighbouring towns of Lisburn and Whitehead.

As with PACE, the movement organised community projects, arranged holidays for families and for those harassed and wearied in the early years of continued rioting and bombing. They ran playgroups for children and collected funds for Mother Teresa's work, for Corrymeela and reconciling project bodies like the Harmony Trust.

On occasions their members took part in more dramatic and courageous actions in Andersonstown and the Ardoyne when they linked arms and formed a human shield to stop youths attacking the army, and in another area they stopped youths from setting fire to property. In yet another incident Women Together members dispersed a gang of youths who were attacking a boy from 'the other side'. As the campaign of violence became better organised with more sophisticated murder weapons, it was not so easy for Women Together to intervene so effectively.

Numerous services and joint prayer meetings were held amongst people who would have considered such activity unthinkable a few years previously. Various activities were held during 1975 to mark International Women's Year, culminating in a large rally in the city centre.

The dead weight of continued violence, when initiative after initiative seems to have failed, has taken its toll of Women Together but they remain in being—in spite of losing all their records and equipment when their office was destroyed by fire. There remains much work for Women Together, especially since the increased polarisation of the communities following hunger-strike deaths.

WITNESS FOR PEACE

The Witness for Peace Campaign was born out of a human tragedy. On 21 July 1972 fourteen-year-old Stephen, the only son of Rev. Joseph and Mrs Parker, was walking along a Belfast street when he was killed by a bomb explosion. He was one of nine killed and 130 injured as a result of 22 Provisional IRA bombs on an afternoon that became known as 'Bloody Friday'.

His father, a Church of Ireland minister in charge of the Mission to Seamen in Belfast, turned his despair at his son's death into a Witness for Peace. He witnessed first of all for three days outside the Belfast City Hall and later repeated the fast outside the General Post Office in Dublin. He felt that he had been guilty of allowing injustices to go unchallenged and invited others to join with him in a consecrational witness.

He collected signatures of those who agreed to make this witness and with the money that was donated he had posters printed which appeared on hoardings in the city and beyond. Car stickers were distributed and Witness for Peace badges sold. He did not really want to start a movement with all the infrastructure of committees and secretaries and minutes, but rather to get as many people as possible to appear publicly as witnesses for peace.

One of his early actions was to call all who had lost a relative in the disturbances to plant a small white cross in the lawn of the City Hall. PACE helped with the organisation and the occasion was marked by a simple ecumenical open air service centred around the 600 white crosses. The ceremony was repeated annually as the numbers killed rose to the 2,000 mark—and the ceremony declined in poignant impact by repetition.

Another original idea met with the same effect. A notice was placed outside the Methodist Church in the central square of Belfast. Thousands passed by daily and had their attention drawn daily to the ever-mounting number who had lost their lives. At least they were reminded initially but as the weeks passed into months and into years the impact was dimmed. When the 2,000 figure was reached the notice was removed.

Joseph Parker collected together six sponsors, Protestants and Catholics, all of whom had lost a relative as a result of the violence. Together with his wife and himself they were to act as Trustees of a fund formed from donations received to be awarded (about £500) annually to an individual or organisation who had made an outstanding contribution to peace.

The first to receive the accolade was the Corrymeela Community in 1975 and the next year a community resource centre in the Ardoyne area of Belfast. Others honoured included Miss Sadie Patterson of Women Together, the surgeon William Rutherford and the Derry Peace Group.

By the time the Trust was formed Joseph Parker had become sad and depressed since enough people would not act positively with him. He was above all disappointed that the backing of his church was so lukewarm and in 1975 he left with his wife to take a church post in Vancouver for the United Church of Canada.

THE GOOD NEIGHBOUR CAMPAIGN

After the rioting and burning of homes in the summer of 1969 a number of peace (keeping) committees had formed themselves in an ad hoc manner in their area. They arranged to keep in touch with the police and the army which had recently come on to the streets for riot control purposes. Usually they had the co-operation of the clergy and the typical pattern was for Protestant and Catholic clerics to stand together outside a pub at closing time and urge men to go home and not do anything foolish. People living in enclaves of 'the other sort' were supported against intimidation wherever possible. These committees met with considerable success, but by the summer of 1970 a relatively quiet winter and spring had weakened their raison d'être, and when in a year or so there was a need for their presence the resurrection proved difficult.

One of the successful Peace Committees of that period had been in East Belfast. However by 1972 the only groups in operation were two PACE groups and a friendship group on the outside of the city of Gilnahirk. This group wrote to the local press in October 1972 and the letter was used as part of a sermon by the Church of Ireland bishop of the diocese. The Gilnahirk Peace Group went on a deputation to the bishop who agreed to call a number of people together to appeal to them to act as Good Neighbours. The ad hoc group formed across the denominational board had a religious flavour along the lines of the catechism teaching that 'my duty towards my neighbour is to love him as myself and to do to all men as I would they should do unto me'.

They were disturbed by seeing neighbours moving out of the area for motives of fear. They wanted not to set up yet another peace organisation, but to get as many citizens in the area as possible to commit themselves towards the establishment of good and intimate neighbourly relationships street by street, and especially to give assurance to those who were living in fear.

Over a period of some three years 10,000 signatories supported such a commitment. In March 1973 the campaign held a conference at Corrymeela which brought together groups from all over the Province. These included the Derry Women of the Creggan (a Londonderry housing estate), Women Together, the Duncairn Friendship Association (another cross-sectarian friendship group based in one area of Belfast) and Action for Peace (see page 115).

The Good Neighbour Campaign also sponsored an East Belfast festival and set up the East Belfast Community Council which remains active and has in fact taken over the main functions of the campaign.

PEACE POINT

After some two years of rioting and bombing it had become patently obvious that it was the violence which made the news and that the 'good news' was lucky to get the bottom third of a column and the three minute radio interview (if the 'bad news' was scarce). The image of life in Northern Ireland was that of a continuous all-embracing civil war, an image as stimulating to the perpetrators of the violence (who gained free publicity thereby) as it was depressing for those who tried to foster constructive enterprises in the Province.

An ad hoc group in Dublin realised this and raised funds to try to publicise the constructive events taking place, particularly in the voluntary sector. A publicity agency was engaged in Belfast to publicise constructive events. This exercise, which must have been costly, resulted in a steady, but rather profligate circulation of press releases which was very pleasing to the organisations concerned, but did not appear to have any marked effect on the media presentation.

For a time a freelance journalist, who had been in the Church, was employed and he made tapes for radio presentation, and published an attractive brochure called *Dovestails*, which gave details of the work of voluntary bodies working in the reconciliation and community field. In all three issues were produced.

Holidays were arranged in the Republic for children from the North and also for the 'Derry Peace Women', who had taken a strong and courageous non-violent stand, long before the women of the Peace People came on the scene. Some tapes were made and sent to a conference held at Amhurst College near Boston. This conference on Northern Ireland's problems was made possible by the generosity of an Irish American and was attended by representatives of a wide range of Northern Ireland organisations, political and otherwise.

A Northern Committee was set up and a part-time organiser appointed. The emphasis tended to move away from direct publicity to the planning of tours for visiting individuals and organisations, particularly from the USA. One of these visits was the 'Pilgrimage of Peace', by 100 Americans who came to share in the Peace People's Boyne Valley rally in December 1976. During the two following summers visits were arranged for groups of Mennonites, who came over in connection with their peace and conflict study courses.

To raise funds a shop was run in Dublin selling secondhand clothes, and others came from American church sources which made it possible to employ a community worker in Belfast for three years.

Peace Point were also interested in the promotion of education and community leadership, and courses were run with the co-operation of Corrymeela covering about 300 people. The courses were run by Dr. Henry Grant, a Jesuit and a scientist who studied counselling psychology in Connecticut for a Master's degree and presented a doctorate thesis at Berkeley, California, on a 'Study of the perspectives of moderate opinion leaders in the Northern Ireland social conflict 1968–75'.

Peace Point no longer operates from a central office and due to lack of funds has had to cut back its activities. Bearing in mind the basic reason for its formation, it should be added as a postscript that towards the end of 1981 a small group came together to print a news-sheet called . . . *And Now the Good News.*

THE PEACE PEOPLE

No other reconciling group attracted as much support or received anything approaching the same world acclaim as the movement which became known as the Peace People. In comparison with other small-scale struggling organisations the Peace People seemed to have all the riches of Aladdin's Cave thrust upon them—the volume of support was such as to be different almost in kind rather than in degree.

Like Witness for Peace, the movement was born out of a tragedy. On 10 August 1976 there had been some IRA disturbances during a march to commemorate the fifth anniversary of internment. A car containing suspects refused to stop at an army road block and was chased up a road leading to Andersonstown, a Republican stronghold. In Finaghy Road North the army opened fire, killing the driver. The car went out of control and mounted the pavement, crushing Mrs Anne Maguire and her three children against some school railings. Two of the children were killed on the spot and the third died in hospital where Anne Maguire remained badly injured.

Betty Williams, a housewife living nearby, was deeply shaken by the event and decided she would organise a petition to call upon the gunmen on both sides to stop. It was time for all mothers and women to say 'Stop'. Anne Maguire's sister, Mairead Corrigan, who worked as a secretary in the office of a large brewery, had been away but returned to hear the terrible news. She also decided to make a public plea to end violence. She asked Ulster Television to give her an opening to make this appeal, and then heard of Betty Williams' petition and the two joined forces.

A meeting was arranged for 14 August just one day after the funeral of the Maguire children. It was held in the grounds of a Catholic church just near the spot where the accident had happened. A short time of prayer and dedication took place and the road was blocked with about 10,000 people present.

The two women were asked to give an interview for Telefis Eireann (of the Republic of Ireland) through a Belfast studio. They arrived too late for the programme and found that a journalist, Ciaran McKeown, had been interviewed instead. He offered his help and the women decided to accept.

It was felt that it should not be 'the women's peace movement' so under Ciaran McKeown's guidance it became 'The Peace People' for whom he wrote a Declaration of Peace. Quite an inspired piece of writing, this declaration, often repeated as a form of public dedication, stood the test of time.

Ciaran McKeown was also engaged in writing a booklet *The Price of Peace*. This was an exhortation to a non-violent way of life which required more courage than the use of the gun. The ideal was a new Northern Ireland, where the citizens co-operated to achieve a prosperous contented Province realising their shared 'Northern Irish' identity. These Northern Irish people were fortunate, he maintained, in having 'a formerly great imperial power which is doggedly refusing to tell us how to live . . . is nevertheless servicing us financially while we evolve our own institutions.' This writing was probably to have more influence outside Northern Ireland than within but the enquiries, requests for interviews, gifts of money came flooding in—to the top floor of the Corrymeela Belfast Centre which had been offered to the Peace People for their use.

Rallies continued, first in the Ormeau Park, Belfast, and at the end of August one which became the Peace People's greatest reconciling triumph. Mainly due to Women Together, under the leadership of Sadie Patterson, an invitation was sent to the Peace People to walk up the Shankill Road, the leading Protestant stronghold, to hold a meeting in Woodvale Park at the top of this long road stretching out from the centre of Belfast. Not one of the 20,000 walking that day could have failed to be moved by the sight of people crowding the pavements clapping as others with banners from all over Belfast and beyond marched along stopping to receive handshakes. Nuns with tears of joy streaming down their faces were welcomed where before they would have been shunned. It looked as if this must be the breakthrough to end violence. It was not the moment for sober reflection—which would have reminded one that every 12 July not 20,000 but 100,000 Orangemen marched through the Province watched by several times that number.

Some of these Orangemen living in the Shankill must have been sceptical at least—if not downright suspicious—of a movement started by three Catholics, but they were content to keep quiet and act as good hosts on that Saturday. If not the status quo, Protestant hardliners had much to gain from peace. It was the extreme Republicans, Provisional IRA, Irish

National Liberation Army and the Irish Socialist Republican Party who had most to fear, for if the Catholic population turned solidly against them it would be very difficult for them to survive and the 'Brits' would remain and so would partition.

The Peace People felt something of this opposition when they visited the Republican housing estate of Turf Lodge. This was a courageous act—a child had recently been hit by a plastic bullet fired by the army and had died. The Peace Women were heckled and manhandled. It was said they were tools of the army and the British. Why did they not direct their attention to the Protestant assassins?

The IRA must have seen the Peace People as something of a threat for on the day of 25 October, when there was to be a peace march up the Falls Road, they held a counter-rally in Falls Park (said to be attended by 2,000 supporters). Some of their supporters went down to an area near a large cemetery and pelted the peace marchers with stones and bits of metal. It was a very wet day and the umbrellas of the marchers gave them some protection. No-one was badly hurt except Sadie Patterson of Women Together who had gone on to a stand inside the Falls cemetery with a gift of money for the Peace People. Some Republicans pulled down the Peace People's posters and, recognising Sadie Patterson, set upon her and knocked her unconscious, and she had to spend a protracted time in hospital as a result. A marcher, used to vigils and marches in the UK, said she was shaken by the anger in the faces of the stoning Republicans, which she had not experienced before. Such is the emotional nature of Northern Ireland's divisions.

The leaders had other things to occupy their minds. If they were not wanted in parts of Belfast other countries competed for their appearance. The three were flown to the USA and back for a television programme. Above all, Norwegians took them to their hearts. The two women were sponsored (jointly by other groups in Germany also) for the Nobel Peace Prize. It was too late for inclusion with the 1976 nominees, but the press in Norway set up a fund for the Peace People and later in the year the leaders returned to Norway to be fêted and given a contribution which finally amounted to £202,000.

Sums of this size automatically create speculation and rumours, but eventually these were in part silenced by the wise announcement that a trust was being formed to be administered by trustees drawn from all sections of the community with Ciaran McKeown as the chairman. Over the next two years grants were made mainly to youth and community projects especially where there was an element of self-help. A proportion went to help small business ventures which appeared to have good prospects and which could give local employment opportunities.

The sums were increased by at least £40,000 from German sources while funds in general flowed in to make it possible for Mairead to join Betty in full time work for the movement. Ciaran McKeown gave up his post as editor of the journal *Fortnight* and was at first sponsored by a Quaker trust and later by the International Peace Research Institute in Oslo.

The movement's journal *Peace by Peace*, well produced and edited by Ciaran McKeown, did not pay for itself but was covered by a grant from an American foundation.

From the capital funds £40,000 was taken to purchase a house to give the movement more space. It was becoming, in terms of any peace movement, quite a large operation. The house was called Fredheim, House of Peace, in honour of the Norwegians whose funds made it possible. Situated in a Protestant area, but on a main artery out of the city it is in a 'neutral' area which gives access to all. It has become a port of call for all overseas visitors interested in the local scene.

Marches were being held for the Peace People in leading cities and in towns throughout the UK, and the leaders were in demand in so many places that other supporters had to help out at times. It was very heady wine, though an exhausting assignment, though to be fair it must be said that the leaders did not shirk difficult tasks at home. *Peace by Peace* was sold on the streets and the leaders knocked on doors of people's homes—even in the areas where extreme Protestants lived. By this time, however, the two women were television personalities and to have them in your home was an honour—even if you did not agree with them.

Obviously rallies and marches could not go on for ever without loss of impact, but there was one last dramatic march which was held in early December 1976. The venue chosen was Drogheda on a recently completed bridge across the Boyne, not far from the site of the famous battle of 1690. Bus loads of supporters came from Northern Ireland, and many others came from groups which had been formed in the Republic. It was a cold, overcast, uninviting day as these groups converged on the bridge from opposite sides of the river. Just as speeches were about to be made the sun burst through. It was as though special divine recognition had been given and the feeling of goodwill seemed especially blessed as people went home cheered, having also heard a song from Joan Baez, a particular friend of the movement. She had been joined by 100 of her countrymen and women who had come over from the USA on a special pilgrimage of peace.

The two Peace Women were mentioned by the Queen in her Christmas television and radio speech and in 1977 a ban on Irish demonstrations in Trafalgar Square (in operation since Bloody Sunday 1972) was lifted to enable the Peace People to meet there. These acts were cited as evidence that the Peace People were British Government agents, but to have prevented a meeting of a non-violent movement in favour of peace in Northern Ireland would have warranted wholesale condemnation. Joan Baez was again with the leaders, on the plinth of Nelson's Column, and although there was organised chanting by Irish Republicans and members of the Troops Out Movement, the Peace People triumphantly carried the day.

Over the next three years Mairead Corrigan and Betty Williams did good work in the USA by urging at all levels a cessation of all funds being sent to Ireland which directly or indirectly would be used to support paramilitary groups. By this time the Noraid Fund supporters were protesting their aid went only for relief of prisoners' families but there was a big question mark here. In Canada Betty Williams also criticised funds being sent to aid Protestant paramilitary groups, though in comparison with Republican support this aid was really insignificant.

As well as penetrating to those in high office, for instance the Speaker of the House of Representatives, T. P. O'Neill, both women faced audiences of Irish Americans who did not take at all kindly to find women, and Catholics to boot, shattering their simplistic conception of Northern Ireland's problem, i.e. that if the wicked British and their army could be got out of the island all would be well.

At home there was an attempt to strengthen and work through local Peace People groups which had been springing up in support. The groups were difficult to count, some sprang up spontaneously, some vanished. It is thought that 60 might be a reasonable estimate at the peak.

The question was now being asked, what type of government did the Peace People want? Ciaran McKeown gave them a lead. The existing political parties were trapped by tribal history, by intransigent manifestos, so scrap the lot and start again, he said. Let each area form their own community group which would send a representative to an assembly, just as the different peace groups sent representatives to the Peace People's Assembly. There would also be an Upper House of nominated representatives from various branches of society, the Church, Education and Learning, the Law and cultural activities.

As soon as you lay down a specific policy it becomes divisive; 'peace' means different things to different people. For example, those who saw a viable political future in the Alliance Party or who were members of the Northern Ireland Labour Party were alienated.

McKeown developed his ideas further, at one point suggesting a Federation of the British Isles. The Community group representation was defined later as a policy of 'cantonisation', each canton to represent about 5,000 people.

Hard on the heels of this Assembly came the presentation of the Nobel Peace Prize and another triumphant trip to Norway. It was no doubt logical to argue that the £80,000 wisely invested would make it possible for Mairead and Betty to work full-time in perpetuity for the Peace People without being a drain on the movement's finances. Unfortunately, that was not the way that many saw it. The detractors of the Peace People, who had been jeering, 'Join the Peace People and see the world', were now able to add that the two women were certainly making a good thing for themselves out of this peace business. If the prize money had been used to fund, for instance, volunteers to go to work for a year in the third world, this would have formed a continuing monument to the Peace People and would have encouraged further giving.

As Nobel Prize laureates, the two women were able to nominate Adolfo Perez Esquivel as a possible recipient for the Peace Prize in 1979. They also petitioned the Argentinian government for the release of this non-violent human rights organiser and Mairead did a good job in visiting some of the non-violent groups in the Argentine to assure them of the support of the Peace People for their cause. When Esquivel finally was released and able to go to Norway to receive his prize, he was invited to come and speak in Northern Ireland, which he did in 1980.

In 1978 the three leaders sensibly decided that the control of the movement should be broadened—for one thing, the three were from the Catholic community. They did not, in fact, stand for election to the Executive Committee. Peter McLachlan was elected chairman and there were other new faces on the Executive. Peter McLachlan had worked for the Conservative Party Research Unit and had been an active member of the Unionist Party of Northern Ireland in the post-Sunningdale Assembly. His wide experience, especially in the sphere of voluntary Housing Associations, gave a new constructive look to the work of the Peace People. He was re-elected chairman in the autumn of 1979, but this time the three leaders were back serving on the Executive.

Ciaran McKeown had in the meantime proposed a change in the Emergency Provisions Act, which would accord a new emergency status to those tried by the Diplock Courts. This, he claimed, would not amount to political status, but would acknowledge that the men of violence were not for the most part ordinary criminals. This campaign had a highly divisive effect on the Peace People.

There must have been further dissension on the Peace People's Executive Committee, for there were various resignations: the vice-chairman, the treasurer and in February 1980, Betty Williams withdrew from the service of the Peace People. Next, one heard that the chairman, Peter McLachlan, had been voted off the Committee and that the chair had been taken by Mairead Corrigan. Some Peace People's groups, where they had not withered away through apathy, reformed themselves to act independently of the Peace People. This, for example, happened in Londonderry and in Sydenham (an East Belfast suburb) and the whole movement appeared to be in complete disarray. Naturally, overseas supporters fell away and one heard of financial difficulties; however, some members have remained faithful. Ciaran McKeown, the former editor of their paper, *Peace by Peace*, disappeared from the councils of the Peace People and the editorship has been taken over by Steve McBride. Representatives of the

Peace People took their place alongside the other minority groups working together in the Peace Forum.

THE PEACE FORUM

Mention has been made of the 1971 Petition for Sanity and the co-operation of a number of movements to organise the Botanic Gardens, Belfast, rally. From time to time representatives of the reconciling groups came together to share their thinking, to report on what each was planning and to invite the support of others in various projects. By 1974 these meetings had been placed on a regular basis with a chairman and a secretary.

The issue of combined publicity was raised on occasions. At each tragedy or significant event, press, radio and television turned to political spokesmen for comment, the voice of the peace-loving citizen was not heard. It was suggested that a representative should be nominated for each group, making up what was to be called 'The Peace Forum', to speak and pronounce on events from the Forum's point of view. One difficulty was that the Forum constituent members represented a wide approach, united by a desire to stop violence—some were pacifist, some were not; some could make political statements, some could not. The argument used, 'if the peace groups can't agree, what hope is there for other sections of the community coming together' did not really represent the situation. The groups did not quarrel, at times joint statements were made and joint projects mounted. This trend has increased in the eighties, but in the mid-seventies there were two attempts to set up umbrella peace movements.

The first was initiated by a Belfast surgeon, William Rutherford, himself a member of the Corrymeela Community. The basic argument sounded logical. The reconciling movements would be so much stronger if they would all work together. To this idea was added the exciting prospect that the new movement would become an Action for Peace in that representatives from all the groups would hold themselves in readiness to go at a moment's notice to support anyone or any group threatened anywhere (within the Belfast area for a start) and by their sheer numbers unarmed would make any physical attack by either side almost impossible. Although some individuals were given individual support, the logistics of such a project, on the scale required for successful operation, made it impossible.

As far as the idea of a blanket peace organisation was concerned, this was not acceptable as most people wanted to work for their own organisation or movement and did not want to hand over control to what appeared to be yet one more reconciliation movement. Those originally interested in the idea continued to meet once a month as Action for Peace.

At this time Harry Murray, who had been a leading figure in the Ulster Workers' Council at the time of the 1974 strike, felt that he, as a Protestant, should hold out the hand of friendship to fellow citizens who were Catholics. He saw this as a consequence of his fundamentalist religious faith. He was supported by Sadie Patterson and also Canon Murphy, a priest whose parish included the Falls Road and the Ballymurphy and Turf Lodge estates, as well as Vivian Simpson (the one remaining Northern Ireland Labour Party member at Stormont at the time of dissolution) and others. It was decided to make a very broad appeal. There was, of course, Women Together, but this was to be the big push that everyone wanted; it was in fact 'People Together'. A mass meeting, held in the Belfast Methodist Grosvenor Hall, with a capacity of 2,000, took place early in 1975. It was well filled and was by far the largest indoor gathering of this type on the issue of the ending of violence. Sadie Patterson was in the chair and Harry Murray was given a standing ovation. There was a queue of people from the floor waiting to speak into the microphone, but there were very noticeably fewer people at the follow-up meeting the next week.

However, a sufficient number of people agreed to mount a campaign and to form groups in different towns. The leaders went round to various provincial towns holding well enough attended meetings, but the vital spark which was to ignite the Peace People some 18 months later was lacking. Most of the organisers of People Together were already committed to other reconciling groups. They could see no point in running yet another body which was not making progress. Finally it was decided to lay the central committee down, much to the disgust of Harry Murray, for it was his original and only peace movement. A group in Lisburn continued to meet as 'People Together' for a time and Harry Murray carried on with his group in Bangor. The balance of the money collected for the work was divided between these two groups.

The Peace Forum began to see its role more clearly and was gaining in strength. So long as there was no question of violating the autonomy of the member organisations, these bodies were often happy to act in concert through the Forum. At the time of the Constitutional Convention all delegates were urged by the Forum to go with an open mind dedicated to finding an agreed form of government (see the notes on the New Ulster Movement) and towards the end of 1975 the member organisations united to help with a city centre rally which Women Together were organising to mark the close of International Women's Year.

The Forum initiated some action itself on behalf of members, a visit to the Northern Ireland Office, and meetings on two occasions with the civil representatives of the army and the police. In August 1980 Lord Elton, the Minister of State responsible for Education, met with the Forum. In October of that year the first of the Forum's Corrymeela Conferences was held. These gave members time to discuss in greater depth their different approaches. In January 1981 another such conference was held where a number of new initiatives were taken back to the member organisations for discussion. After the death of the hunger strikers in 1981 the Forum realised the pressure under which non-violent community workers in Catholic areas in Belfast were working. They were specially invited to a Forum open house to meet in a neutral and relaxed atmosphere and discuss their problems. It was agreed to repeat this experiment.

In 1981 organisations outside the Belfast area were also invited to come to the Forum meetings. The representatives from Londonderry in particular had experiences somewhat different from those met with in Belfast, the sharing of which was of mutual benefit. In 1982 the Forum felt strong enough to engage, with the help of a government employment scheme, a full-time organiser. The increased tensions of 1981 served to draw the reconciling movements closer together and to establish the place of the Peace Forum more securely in their thinking and planning.

7 Alternative forms of government

As we have seen, the proroguing of Stormont came as a considerable shock to most people in Northern Ireland. Ever since it was clear that the Boundary Commission in 1925 was not proposing any drastic truncating of the Northern Ireland territory, the Province assumed, as the years went by, an increasing image of permanence.

To Protestants it was 'our Ulster', securely linked to the British throne. It was not emotionally satisfying to Catholics, but many accepted its continuance for a number of years as inevitable. In fact, according to a survey commissioned by the *Belfast Telegraph* in December 1967, only 37% of Catholics in their sample wanted a United Ireland separated from Great Britain.[1]

They were influenced, no doubt, by the better state health, social security and pension amenities than those available in the South. Considerable upgrading of social security and pension rates in the Republic in recent years, however, has gone a considerable way to closing the gap.

However, with continued violence, with the defeat of the Power-Sharing Executive and the failure of the Constitutional Convention in 1975 to achieve a consensus, the whole political future of Northern Ireland is now in the melting pot. It is therefore a worthwhile exercise to review all alternatives, if for no other reason than to discard those which provide no hope of sufficient general agreement and to channel constructive thought along lines which have some hope of achieving consensus.

Integration with Britain

Throughout the protracted Home Rule debates before the First World War, the northern Unionists made it quite clear that continued rule from Westminster—for the whole island—was what was wanted. Northern Ireland as a separate state was a second best. It thus may appear curious that Loyalists do not now call for complete integration.

In 1936 the annual report of the Unionist Standing Committee stated, 'Northern Ireland without a parliament of her own would be a standing temptation to certain British politicians to make another bid for a final settlement with Irish Republicans.'[2] The 'Republicans' of those days were De Valera's Fianna Fail government, not the IRA, but one can hear an echo today in the response, in some quarters, to the Conservative Government's 1980 talks with the Republic.

Northern Protestants have experienced their own Home Rule for over half a century, and some loyalty to the devolved state has been forged. To lose this privilege was seen as a step down. Northern Ireland is a relatively small area compared to Great Britain, its population only 2.7% of the rest of the UK, and it cannot claim much time in the Westminster programme, where it generates little interest, except on some security issues.

Finally, Westminster no longer represents the great imperial power which automatically claimed loyalty from Northern Protestants. This change is now coupled with the poor economic showing during recent years.

Enoch Powell, Unionist MP for South Down, alone remains wedded to full integration, but he could scarcely be regarded as a typical Ulster Unionist, but more as a 'guest star' or by some as a cuckoo in the nest. The Democratic Unionist Party has at times stood for integration; more recently this line has been dropped and a return to the 1968 Stormont would, for its members, be a more desirable arrangement.

Nationalists, obviously, see such a close link with Britain as an undesirable step, although it would serve as a reasonable insurance against any return to discriminatory practices.

There are now signs that public opinion in Great Britain has no great desire to be completely integrated with such an intransigent problem. Patience may be wearing thin.

Because of the wide range of powers transferred to Stormont, a representation of 12 MPs at Westminster was considered reasonable, although a true representation on a proportional basis works out at 17. Prior to partition the six northern counties were over-represented, with 30 seats, and it was the Redistribution of Seats (Ireland) Act 1918, which cut the number to 13. The thirteenth seat was a Queen's University representative, which was lost in 1948 along with the British University representation. It was agreed in March 1979 that the electoral Boundary Commission be given the power to vary the Northern Ireland constituencies to contain between 16 and 18 and to make recommendations. Labour governments were not anxious to make this adjustment because regularly 10 or 11 of the Northern Ireland MPs elected were Unionists who usually (though not exclusively) voted with the Conservative Party. During the periods of very slender Labour majorities these votes became at times crucial. The Labour argument against a proportional Northern Ireland representation was that, while the Unionist MPs claimed the right as members of the House of Commons to vote on all issues, they strenuously maintained that matters which fell within the constitutional competence of the Northern Ireland Parliament should be discussed only within the Northern Ireland House. This was a position readily agreed to by earlier parliaments at Westminster, when members had no desire to be drawn into local issues which they did not fully understand, yet knew were fraught with complications. After the events of 1968 it was argued that this policy showed a reprehensible lack of responsibility, since Westminster was ultimately responsible for the government of the Province, a right they claimed in 1972 when proroguing Stormont.

Nationalists were in general against the increase of representation which, even if it might give them one or two extra seats at Westminster, would serve to strengthen the British link.

Direct Rule

The proroguing of Stormont was followed by the Northern Ireland (Temporary Provisions) Act in 1972. This Act was extended until 1973, when it was replaced by a Northern Ireland Constitution Act which provided for a 78-member Assembly to be elected by proportional representation. The election was to take place on 28 June 1973, and the power of control passed again to the Northern Ireland-based Assembly on 1 January 1974.

It was this Act which substituted this Assembly for the Parliament of Northern Ireland. It was also this Act which terminated the office of the Governor of Northern Ireland. Section 1 of the Constitution Act stated 'It is hereby declared that Northern Ireland remains part of Her Majesty's dominions and of the UK and it is hereby affirmed that in no event will Northern Ireland or any part of it cease to be part of Her Majesty's dominions and of the UK without the consent of the majority of the people in Northern Ireland voting in a poll held for the purposes of this section in accordance with Schedule 1 of this Act.'

When the Northern Ireland Assembly was prorogued following the fall of the Executive in 1974, a new Northern Ireland Act was passed, handing power back to the Secretary of State assisted by a team of junior ministers. The Act also provided for the holding of a Constitutional Convention, and when the Convention was finally dissolved on 5 March 1979 Direct Rule continued to operate.

Direct Rule means that control of Northern Ireland is vested in Westminster through the Secretary of State, who has a seat in the Cabinet. It does not mean that all local legislation is automatically repealed or that all UK legislation applies. The fact that so much of the Stormont legislation was a replica of Westminster Acts (the 'Step by Step' policy) means that citizens of Northern Ireland live under very similar legislation to the rest of the UK.

There are some areas where it remains different from England and Wales—as happens in Scotland. The death penalty, for instance, can be applied for killing a policeman (this no longer applies—May 1982—editor), licensing laws regarding the sale of alcohol are different, and so is the position of homosexuals, and on this issue both Protestants and Catholics have resisted bringing the law into line with the rest of the UK.

As has been seen, Northern Protestants constituted a recalcitrant minority willing to fight against their own alleged 'family'—Britain—rather than agree to be ruled from Dublin.

Lloyd George, the premier at the time, said of these Protestants in 1918 that they were:

> 'as alien in blood, in religious faith, in traditions, in outlook—as alien from the rest of Ireland in this respect as the inhabitants of Fife or Aberdeen . . . To place them under national rule against their will would be a glaring outrage on the principle of liberty and self-government as the denial of self-government would be to the rest of Ireland.'[5]

Functional co-operation North and South had been developing healthily, if slowly, in the fifties and sixties, and looked for a while, with O'Neill at the helm, as though it might flourish officially at top level. However, the fear of the Republic remained in the Protestant tribal subconscious, not far from the surface.

With the onslaught of the Provisionals' campaign of violence this fear became very real, and it put back North/South co-operation for years. This violence came at a time when, as fellow members of the European Economic Community, close co-operation could have been of benefit to both parties.

It has not been forgotten in the North that the 1937 Constitution of the Republic still stands. This constitution, framed at the behest of Eamonn De Valera's government, finally ended any thought that the Free State was a dominion. Its name was changed to Ireland, or, officially in Irish, Eire. The break was completed in 1949, curiously enough not by the Fianna Fail government, but by the less Republican opposition, Fine Gael, with John A. Costello as Taoiseach. Eire left the Commonwealth and became the Republic of Ireland.

Article 2 of the constitution states: 'The national territory consists of the whole island of Ireland, its islands and territorial waters', and Article 3—'Pending the re-integration of the national territory and without prejudice to the right of the Parliament and Government established by the Constitution to exercise jurisdiction'. These clauses remain as an ultimate threat to Northern Protestants.

It is true that in 1972 Article 44 Subsection 5 was revoked by a national referendum. The Article stated that 'the State recognises the special position of the Holy Catholic Apostolic and Roman Church as the guardian of the Faith professed by the great majority of the citizens'. But whether or not the Catholic Church has official backing matters little if the population accept its teaching. The government is not likely to do anything contrary to the Church's teachings where 95% of the population belong to that Church.

The indications are that the government of the Republic (no matter which party was in power) would be highly embarrassed if by some remote chance the northern counties wished to repudiate partition and accept the jurisdiction of the Republic. The Republic would take on an industrial economy with a high unemployment level approaching 20% and receiving at the time of writing a subvention of over £1,000 million per annum. It has been estimated that if such a subvention was to be met from the Irish exchequer, it would require (1979/80 figures) almost a 50% increase in the Republic's tax bill.[6] Even given the Republic's good economic progress in the seventies and the advantages reaped by the farming community through EEC subsidies, this is a daunting figure, especially in view of the Republic's heavy state borrowing in recent years.

It is fair to state that, unless stirred up by some emotive act such as 'Bloody Sunday' or the deaths of hunger strikers, the citizens of the Republic are not particularly interested in 'the black north'. To suggest in a referendum that their country should renounce its claim to the northern counties might well invoke just such a stirring emotion to swing the scales appreciably against any such change, a factor which the Prime Minister in office in 1981 must take into his calculations if contemplating a constitutional change.

In the past the Catholic birth rate has been higher than that of Protestants. At the moment there are in Northern Ireland as many Catholic children at primary schools as there are Protestants. From 1937 to 1961 the Catholic one-third of the population gave rise to 56% of the emigrants going to Great Britain and further afield. This was just enough to drain off the excess births in the Catholic community and leave the proportions static.[7] From the 1971 figures it looks as if the Catholic proportion is increasing.

The surgeon John H. Robb maintains that one day the Protestants will find themselves in a minority position. As a Protestant himself he argues that Protestants should call from strength and make reasonable provision in a United Ireland for what they hold dear. He feels that they have a valuable contribution to make to a United Ireland and hopes that they will be integrated with the rest of the population and will come to identify with them.

It is one thing to accept that if a majority in the North desired such unity that Britain would not stand in the way—and this needs to be said, if only to clear away any misapprehension that Britain and the British army maintain partition to serve their own ends. It is another thing for any leading party in Britain to maintain it is working towards such an end—in the hope of eventually obtaining the full co-operation of Protestants. Such a declaration would evoke Protestant suspicion, and every subsequent act by Britain would require to be scrutinised in case it is geared to bring about directly or indirectly the demise of the Protestant state.

Federation

If Irish unity is not to be, one looks, therefore, at some constitutional arrangement which would increase the bonds between North and South and still give protection and limited autonomy to the million Protestants.

Some form of federation, or less tightly bound confederation springs to mind. With a federation the federal government is the main unit: some autonomy is agreed to be the right of the separate states or constituent units comprising the federation. The United States and the Swiss Federation are obvious examples.

With a confederation the separate states are the continuing autonomous units which agree to hand over to a central government certain defined and limited issues. There is a sense in which the European Economic Community is a confederation covering certain financial, economic and Customs issues. If the Council of Ireland had been able to operate, then limited power to make binding decisions might be vested in the Council and to that extent would bring the island within the bounds of becoming a confederation.

Regarding Northern Ireland, economic questions require an answer. Who is going to pay the subsidies, grants, unemployment and social security commitments currently met by the British exchequer? Presumably in such a federation it is assumed that a break is to be made from Britain. Is it being assumed that Britain, heaving a sigh of relief at being freed from the burden of administering Northern Ireland, would be willing to continue, at least for a time, to meet most of these subventions?

If too much autonomy is given to the 'Ulster State' government then the Catholic community will risk being continually outvoted. If all real power rests with the Federal Government, then in Ireland the State of Ulster will be outvoted.

A federal Ireland is the solution proposed by the Provisional Sinn Fein. Under their scheme the old nine-county Province of Ulster would become one of the four State Governments in the 'Eire Nua'. It is difficult to see why the Republic would wish to cut its territory into three State Governments, Leinster, Munster and Connaught, just to suit this plan, when there is no such local desire for these measures of provincial autonomy. If this plan still finds favour with the Provisional IRA very little is heard of it, while their campaign is directed to severing the link with Britain.

If the proposed devolution for Scotland and Wales had been accepted in 1979 then a similar pattern for Northern Ireland might have completed the picture with Westminster emerging as a form of Federal Government for the United Kingdom.

Whether the Republic of Ireland would eventually join a Confederation of the British Isles is another question. Economically speaking such a plan would have much to commend it. If such a confederation controlled only limited spheres of operation, then the Republic would not be in the same position as in a federation, where her representatives would always be liable to be in a minority whatever the basis of representation.

In any case the Republic of Ireland has carved a special place for her representatives at the United Nations, and in the European Parliament and the various conferences and agencies that comprise the European Economic Community. These would not be lightly given up.

When a community is swayed by nationalistic emotions, the sober reasoning of everyday living can make little headway. If the emotions recede, the need to have an occupation to justify oneself and to feed and care for one's family begins to take its proper place. The way would then be open to a sober approach to new fields of co-operation without upsetting any existing constitutional arrangements, and to the benefit of all parties concerned, including Northern Ireland.

Northern Ireland as an independent state

The concept of Northern Ireland existing without constitutional ties with Britain or the Republic has been mooted from time to time although little attention was given to the idea until the seventies.

The frustration of the continuing violence and the failure of the army to stamp out the Provisional IRA and other Republican paramilitary bodies has probably led more people to give independence serious thought. There is also the feeling that the Protestant Loyalists' first loyalty is to the maintenance of the Northern Ireland State. As has been mentioned the Crown no longer represents an imperial power and cannot claim quite the same respect as an institution no matter how popular members of the Royal Family may be. In spite of the repeated assurances of support for the continuation of Northern Ireland as a part of the United Kingdom, the realisation that the Province is a financial drain on a hard-pressed economy leaves some Protestants with the uneasy feeling that Westminster might change its mind.

There is also in the face of Britain's economic showing, the query whether after all Northern Ireland might not do better on her own. From 1908 to 1974 the productivity of Northern Ireland continued to increase at a greater rate than in the rest of the UK and to stand up very well to the bombing and violence. The Republic's economy made creditable advances in the seventies. Northern Ireland, it was argued, should be able to do likewise.

These ideas found their most persuasive backers from a group which emerged from former Protestant extremists. Disillusioned with the use of violence as a response to Republicanism they set up an organisation called the New Ulster Political Research Group. The existence of the Catholic minority with a different cultural identity is recognised but not felt to be an insurmountable hurdle.

A carefully prepared Bill of Rights is seen as giving the minority all necessary protection and the proposed constitution and form of government draws heavily on the United States pattern. This group appears to have broken up in 1981 and its Belfast office to have closed down.

On the concept of a Bill of Rights there is sound backing from the Standing Advisory Commission on Human Rights.[8] This body, independent but set up by the Northern Ireland Constitution Act 1973, has produced a Bill of Rights which it argues should be applied to the UK as a whole. This would bring the UK into line with the EEC and enable citizens to have recourse at home to alleged injustices, without having to take their case to the European Commission in Strasbourg.

The Advisory Commisson envisages such a Bill of Rights operating as an addition to the existing British political and legal system, and which would ultimately operate with any devolved government. Whether such a Bill operating in an independent Northern Ireland context would give the Catholic community sufficient assurance is open to question.

Others would see the break with Britain as a dangerous move on three counts. First of all many Protestants have a deep traditional loyalty to the British Crown and way of life. The link is not just a 'marriage of convenience'. To break with this would mean a loss of heritage. Secondly some would fear that without the backing of Britain, Northern Ireland might be swallowed up by the Republic. The fact that statements have been made on a number of occasions by the leaders of governments in the Republic that Ireland will not be united by force does not alter the fears of those who hold them traditionally.

Thirdly, and more realistically, there are serious doubts as to whether it is reasonable to expect Northern Ireland to exist as a viable economic unit without the UK financial backing in 1982 in the region of £1,000 million per annum. It might be possible to make an arrangement with Britain to phase out the subsidies only gradually. It is a stimulating thought that an Ulster in business on its own account could release a flood of new-found energy and enterprise. Whether in this capital-intensive, automated age such enterprise could soak up the large numbers of unemployed workers, or could find a substitute for subventions amounting to over a quarter of Northern Ireland's locally generated income is highly doubtful.[9]

Oil under Lough Neagh, natural gas off the coast of County Down, might change matters! If a state can go some way to feeding itself, its smallness (as has been seen) may, of itself, not matter. In Northern Ireland, however, the citizens would have to be willing to tighten their belts, suffer direction of labour, face productivity targets, six-day weeks, rationing of petrol and restriction of travel outside the territory. It is doubtful whether the people of Northern Ireland are willing to pay this price. From a 1979 opinion survey it would appear that only 1% of the population see an independent Northern Ireland as its preferred constitutional solution.[10]

A declaration of intent

The principal stated aim of the Provisional IRA is that Britain should make a firm declaration of intent to withdraw from Northern Ireland. Clearly the longer the period involved the less likely the acceptance by the Provisionals. If they could claim this intended withdrawal as 'victory' the campaign of violence would be, at least for a period, terminated.

To give the world this example of protracted violence as a successful way of gaining political results would be a sad blow to all those working for reconciliation and peaceful change throughout the world. There is every chance that it would not result in lasting peace. To believe otherwise is to ignore the attitude of the Protestant majority.

Whether Ian Paisley's February 1981 claim to be able to rally 150,000 armed men is an exaggerated claim or not, it can be taken that the Protestant 'Third Force' would be formidable. The more that Protestants feel threatened the more their paramilitary organisations become 'legitimised' as the defence force of the majority.

Faced with the frustrating deadlock between the leading political parties it is understandable that the argument has been put forward that if Britain should withdraw, both sides would have to sit down and thrash out some way of living together. The Unionist Party, the argument runs, secure in the knowledge that Northern Ireland remains a part of the UK, will not agree to any form of shared devolved government. Similarly, it is argued, the SDLP spokesmen push their demands further than is reasonable, knowing that the British Government is there to prevent unbridled Protestant rule.

The SDLP has, however, asked Great Britain to withdraw the guarantee to remain in Northern Ireland as long as the majority wish it. The aim is to get the Unionist Party to make concessions in a negotiated devolved government agreement.

There is a sense in which the existence of a million determined British citizens in Northern Ireland is the best guarantee of the link in itself. If the removal of the guarantee means anything, it is as a form of threat to the majority. If they do not do what they are told they may be abandoned. Such a reversal of policy would, as has been noted, be regarded by Protestants as a treacherous act. It would encourage still further the formation, by extreme Loyalist organisations, of groups of armed men, organised to take over should such a withdrawal take place.

Devolved government

The above arguments lead to the final possibility, that is, some type of devolved government. The Stormont regime, operating under the Government of Ireland 1920 Act, was a form of devolution which operated for 51 years. In 1972 it was prorogued, not dissolved, but at the present time it could not be reinstated exactly as before, even though provision might be made to have the recent reforms made permanent. Such a large nationalist opposition, denied, ad infinitum, a say in any legislation, would not agree to this straightforward majority rule.

Before the whole workings of 'Stormont' are written off with the glib phrase 'Fifty years of mis-rule' it should be said that Central Government and the Civil Service functioned well, fairly and efficiently, even though Catholics were badly under-represented in all its ranks.[11]

It was at the level of local government that discrimination was at times blatant. It was within the power of local councils to build and allocate houses for renting, to grant positions of employment in state schools, in the council offices and statutory local services. The best positions usually went with the patronage of the controlling party. Of the 73 local authorities there were 11 rural or urban councils controlled by Nationalist majorities where Catholics tended to come off best. There were therefore 61 Unionist-controlled bodies where the opposite was the case. The fact that in seven of these, three towns and four rural districts, Catholic voters were actually in the majority, caused very bitter feeling.[12]

The Central Government was at fault in not checking these abuses. Apart from acquiescing in and at times aiding the alteration of ward boundaries in provincial towns to produce an undemocratic result, other steps could have been taken. Belfast County Borough had a points system to ensure the fair allocation of houses. It worked well. It could have been made mandatory for all local authorities.

In general administration the record was good. The Ministry of Agriculture served the farming community well. The main industry of the Province was supported in research, training, standard maintenance and subsidies. The Ministry of Commerce induced many overseas firms to come to Northern Ireland and built a number of advance factories in anticipation. The west and the periphery did not benefit proportionately here, but firms naturally preferred the more accessible areas. Stormont found the Ulster schools in a parlous state; the Ministry of Education left the Province's educational system in an exemplary state. More liberal grants were made to voluntary schools (including all Catholic schools) than are made in Great Britain.

The system of devolved government has much to commend it. Latterly Brian Faulkner experimented by inviting first a member of the Northern Ireland Labour Party and later a non-Party Catholic to join his Cabinet,

1971/2, for the statutory limit of six months. He proposed the formation of committees to advise on legislation and suggested that the chairmen of some of these could be drawn from the minority. It was too little and too late but it showed the direction that devolved government could take.

It was taken much further by the 1974 Assembly of 78 members and the Power-Sharing Executive. It was a tragedy that events conspired to bring to an end this experiment before it really had time to prove its worth. It was unfortunate that the Executive had thrust upon it the 'Irish dimension' of the proposed Council of Ireland. This measure would have come better later, as a result of functional co-operation between the North and the South.

A joint committee might well have been set up to watch over and organise such joint ventures as energy sharing, tourist development, the fishing industry, and other issues arising as a result of common membership of the European Economic Community.

Forms of coalition do function elsewhere in divided communities. Cross party government operated successfully in Austria from 1945 to 1966 between the two main parties, the Catholics and the Social Democrats. In Switzerland government coalition has become a permanent feature: Here citizens elect members to a National Council or Lower House for a period of four years. In turn the National Council elects on a proportional representation basis, a Federal Council or Government of seven members to serve for four years. These members do not have to be elected members of the National Council, in fact, if they are Council members they have to resign in order to serve in the Government. They cannot be dismissed nor can they dismiss the Council or the Upper House both of which they have the right to address. There is no Prime Minister, but a Chairman whose office rotates annually. The Government is composed of members from three or four parties who work together to initiate legislation. Between differences among themselves or the Cabinet getting at loggerheads with the two Councils it is hard to conceive of a system less likely to succeed. Yet the fact is that it does work in Switzerland and has worked since 1948.[13]

In the Canadian State of New Brunswick there is an interesting comparison to be made with Northern Ireland regarding divisions in the population. The division in this case is ethnic, i.e. French 'Arcadians' comprise 37% of the population. Most Arcadians have French as a mother tongue, though recently English has crept into general use and is now the mother tongue of 12½% of this sub-culture. They are mostly Catholics and their number has been augmented, in the denominational sense, by Catholic immigrants from the USA and elsewhere who speak English. The Catholic proportion of the State population is 52%.

The situation is made easy in comparison with Northern Ireland, because only 25% of the Arcadians (i.e. 9¼% of the State population) definitely wish to be linked to the French speaking neighbouring State of Quebec. In other words there are in New Brunswick a number of cross-cutting allegiances whereas the Northern Ireland divisions remain so stubbornly congruent. In the New Brunswick situation members of the minority groups have been invited to become members of the Cabinet and the results have been beneficial in maintaining harmony in a divided State.[14]

There are other methods of overcoming divisions which might be applied in a devolved Northern Ireland government. One of these is the Belgian method. The divisions here are deep and there has been street violence as well as endless linguistic problems. The French speaking Walloons comprise 40% of the population and 60% are Flemings—speaking Flemish understood in Holland. Various accommodations have been agreed—where a town has two names both appear, and both languages are used in the telephone book. The Council of Ministers must give parity between the linguistic groups, whatever the representation in the House.

Each group is given the right to refer back any measure provided 75% of its members are against it. This does not say that Parliament will alter the bill, but at least it provides a delaying veto which forces Parliament to have a look at the proposed amendments.

The Westminster system works well in Great Britain where parties alternate in power. There is no reason why it should be slavishly followed, especially where the alternation does not take place. There are other possible alternatives, and John Oliver, a former Stormont Permanent Secretary, has made a useful evaluation of some of these.[15] One is the method of weighted majority voting. If a measure is to pass, then the Government is required to have a 75% majority, the aim being to ensure that the bill is acceptable to at least some of the minority. The percentage could if necessary be lower if the previous figure tended to hold up legislation unreasonably. Alternatively it might be made to apply only to certain items such as the election of the Speaker, a finance bill, or the Second Reading of all bills. If the Government was completely blocked then it might be necessary to obtain a waiver of the rule from the Queen's representative or other agreed authority.

The other idea is to have a different type of cabinet structure. By dividing the cabinet into two sections one could be made up of members in charge of a department, say, section 'B'. Here there could be power-sharing, with some leaders of the departments being members of the minority. Section 'A' would be a smaller group elected by a straight majority and this section could guard the constitution. Assured of control of the constitutional position and possibly if given control of the annual estimates, the Unionists could then feel more free to accept shared decisions on other matters. Such an assurance should allow relations to be built up with the Republic of Ireland without the nagging fear of any 'take-over bid'.

Finally one should not overlook the fact that the Alliance Party has 'built-in' power-sharing, its membership and District Council representation being about equally balanced Protestant and Catholic. The attitude survey carried out by the Queen's University Group in May 1979 under the direction of E. P. Moxon-Browne showed that the Alliance Party was the second strongest party in the Province after the Official Unionist Party. This result was obtained by asking the question 'which of the parties do you feel closest to?' The Official Unionists claimed 39.4% of the respondents, but Alliance polled 19.5%, to 17.1% SDLP and 11.8% in support of Paisley's Democratic Unionist Party.[16]

How people in Northern Ireland say they might vote and how they actually do vote may well be two quite different matters. Certainly it has been seen that heightened tension and a heated climate of public opinion increase votes for the more extreme parties at the expense of those at the moderate centre. The deaths of the hunger strikers will not be forgotten, neither will the assassination of Robert Bradford, but emotional heat diminishes fairly rapidly. The increased polarisation does not help the formation of a devolved Northern Ireland Assembly, but such a parliament with safeguards for the minority, and some right to share in the legislation, remains the best hope for the future.

References and notes

Chapter 1

[1] Moody, T. W. 'The Ulster Question 1603 – 1963.' p.7.

[2] Details of employment analyses per denomination in government and the private sector appear in a number of works. The writer offers the original studies made by Charles F. Carter and himself and published in 'The Northern Ireland Problem', 1962 (and republished with editions as a paperback in 1972).

For a comprehensive study of the position see J. H. Whyte, 'How much discrimination was there under the Unionist regime 1921 – 1968?' Contemporary Irish Studies Vol. 1. No. 1. University of Bradford. Summer 1982.

[3] The Civil Authority (Special Powers) Act (Northern Ireland) 1922 was described by Professor F. H. Newark as 'a desperate measure taken to deal with a desperate situation' ('Ulster under Home Rule', ed. T. Wilson, p.50), i.e. the civil war situation at the time. The Minister of Home Affairs was given very wide powers to issue 'all such orders as may be necessary for preserving the peace'. The Act was renewed annually each year until 1933, when it was rendered permanent. The regulations have been altered over the years, but they have given powers to the police to stop, interrogate and search persons and houses, without warrant, on suspicion. The police can also hold such persons for an indefinite period without charge or trial.

Chapter 4 explains how these powers have been altered under Direct Rule.

[4] Changes were to be made under five headings:

1. All local authorities were to publish a readily understood scheme for the allocation of houses.
2. An Ombudsman was to be appointed to investigate grievances in central government administration.
3. The business vote in local government elections (an extra vote for each £10 of valuation of limited companies for rating purposes, up to a maximum of six) was to be abolished forthwith, and within three years a comprehensive reform and modernisation of local government would take place.
4. The Special Powers Act was to be reviewed as soon as conditions allowed and clauses conflicting with international obligations withdrawn from use.
5. The Londonderry City Council was suspended and a Development Commission appointed for three years, charged with the advancement of industrial development and house building.

[5] Bro. the Rev. M. W. Dewar, 'Why Orangeism?' J. H. Jordan. Belfast. 1958. p.23.

[6] 'Violence in Ireland: A report to the Churches.' Joint Study Group. Irish Council of Churches/Roman Catholic Hierarchy. Christian Journals. 1976.

[7] Pope John Paul II, Drogheda. 29 September 1981.
'To all of you who are listening I say: do not believe in violence; do not support violence. It is not the Christian way. It is not the way of the Catholic Church.

. . . to all men and women engaged in violence. I appeal to you in language of passionate pleading. On my knees I beg you to turn away from the paths of violence and to return to the ways of peace. You may claim to seek justice. I too believe in justice and seek justice. But violence only delays the day of justice. Violence destroys the work of justice.'

Chapter 2

[1] Prof. E. E. Evans. 'The Northern Heritage'. *Aquarius*. No. 4. 1971. pp.51-56.
[2] Ciaran McKeown. 'The Price of Peace.' September 1976. Belfast.

Chapter 3

[1] Northern Ireland Constitutional Proposals. H.M.S.O. (London), Cmd. 5259, March 1973.
[2] W. B. Faulkner, MP. First policy speech in the Northern Ireland Assembly as Chief Executive. 24 January 1974. Quoted 'Faulkner—conflict and consent in Irish Politics'. D. Bleakley. Mowbrays, 1974. pp.186-196.
[3] Ibid. p.195.
[4] See R. Fisk, 'The Point of No Return' (for a detailed study of the Strike). London Times Books. Andre Deutsch. 1974.
[5] Op. cit. (see note 2).
[6] 'Northern Ireland—Constitutional Convention: Procedure.' Discussion Paper 2. November 1974. Northern Ireland Office H.M.S.O. (Belfast), paragraph 45. subsections (a) and (c).
[7] Ibid. Foreword by M. Rees, MP, Secretary of State for Northern Ireland.

Chapter 4

[1] Report of the Commission on Disturbances in Northern Ireland. H.M.S.O. (Belfast), Cmd. 532, 1969. The Cameron Report.
[2] Report of Tribunal of Inquiry on violence and civil disturbances in Northern Ireland in 1969. H.M.S.O. (Belfast), Cmd. 566, 1972. The Scarman Report.
[3] Report of the enquiry into allegations against the security forces of physical brutality in Northern Ireland arising out of events on 9 August 1971. H.M.S.O. (London), Cmd. 4823, 1971. The Compton Report.
[4] Report of the Committee of Privy Councillors appointed to consider authorised procedure for the interrogation of persons suspected of terrorism. H.M.S.O. (London), Cmd. 4901, 1972. The Parker Report.
[5] Report of the Tribunal appointed to inquire into the events on Sunday 30 January 1972 which led to the loss of life in connection with the procession in Londonderry on that day, by the Rt. Hon. Lord Widgery OBE, TD. H.M.S.O. (London), HL 101, HG 220, 1972.
[6] Boyle, K., Hadden, T., Hillyard, P., 'Law and State—the Case of Northern Ireland'. Martin Robertson. 1975. pp.91-3.

[7] Report of the Commission to consider legal procedures to deal with terrorist activities in Northern Ireland. H.M.S.O. (London), Cmd. 5185, 1972. The Diplock Report.

[8] For a detailed study of the whole area of administration of justice, carefully documented and containing original study, see 'Ten Years on in Northern Ireland; the legal control of political violence', K. Boyle, T. Hadden and P. Hillyard. Cobden Trust, 1980.

[9] Official Government figures.

[10] Report of a Committee to consider, in the context of civil liberties and human rights, measures to deal with terrorism in Northern Ireland. H.M.S.O. (London), Cmd. 5847, 1975. The Gardiner Report.

[11] The Geneva Conventions of 1949 ruled that guerrillas and resistance fighters must comply with four conditions if they wish to be regarded as combatants:
1. They must be under the control of a commander.
2. Their clothing must show that they are military.
3. They must carry their arms openly.
4. They must obey the laws and customs of war.

[12] The Gardiner Report, p.5.

[13] Report of the committee of inquiry into police interrogation procedures in Northern Ireland. H.M.S.O. (London), Cmd. 7497, 1979. The Bennett Report.

[14] Police Complaints Board for Northern Ireland. Annual Report 1980.

[15] The five demands were:
1. No requirement to undertake prison work.
2. Right of association with other prisoners.
3. Right to wear own personal clothing at all times.
4. Restoration of remission of sentence.
5. Right to send and receive a weekly letter, a weekly parcel and visit.

Chapter 5

[1] RUC Statistics.

[2] 'Flight' Belfast study for Northern Ireland Community Relations Commission, 1971, published 1974.

[3] J. Darby and G. Morris, 'Intimidation in Housing'. Northern Ireland Community Relations Commission, 1974.

[4] See 'Northern Ireland Problem', op. cit. Chapter 6, pp.93-108. Also Joan Darby, 'Conflict in Northern Ireland'. 1976, pp.70-73, 146-151.

[5] Fourth Report of the Fair Employment Agency for Northern Ireland, 1 April 1979–31 March 1980. H.M.S.O. (Belfast), p.290, 7 May 1981.

[6] Annual Report of the Northern Ireland Commissioner for Complaints for 1980, H.M.S.O. (London), p.351, 24 June 1981.

[7] Nos. of insured employees.

	June 1949	*June 1969*
Agriculture	29,900	11,320
Shipbuilding, Marine Engineering	27,500	9,700
Textiles	73,151	49,850

Ulster Year Books

[8] Eileen Evason, 'Ends that won't meet'. Child Poverty Action Group, 1980.

[9] Final Report of the Northern Ireland Supplementary Benefits Commission, Nov. 1980, p.32. After this date the Commission's function was included in the UK Social Security Committee.

[10] See E. A. Aunger, 'In Search of Political Stability: a comparative study of New Brunswick and Northern Ireland', McGill, 1981, p.90, and by the same author, 'Religion and occupational class in Northern Ireland'. *Economic and Social Review*, 1975, No. 7, pp.1-18.

[11] Fourth Report of the Fair Employment Agency for Northern Ireland, 7 May 1981, Cmd. 290, pp.12–14.

[12] J. Darby and J. Williamson, 'Violence and the Social Services in Northern Ireland', 1978, p.12.

[13] E. Deane, 'Community Work in the 70's', in 'Community Work in a Divided Society', ed. H. Fraser. Farset Co-operative Press, 1981, p.9.

[14] M. Fraser, 'Children in Conflict'. Pelican Books, 1973, and in *Community Forum*. Vol. 2, No. 2, 1972, pp.8-9.
H. A. Lyons, 'The Psychological Effects of the Civil Disturbances on Children'. *Northern Teacher*, Winter, 1972.

[15] Ruth Overy, 'Children's Play'. *Community Forum*, Vol. 2, No. 2, 1972, p.10; and see 'Violence in Ireland', op. cit. Chapter 2.

[16] T. Hadden, 'Teacher Training'. *Fortnight*, May 1980, No. 176, p.15.

[17] Lord Chilver's Higher Education Review Group Report, published 5 November 1981, proposed closing the two Catholic teacher training colleges, merging them with the state college. The proposal led to strenuous Catholic opposition.

Chapter 6

[1] A. McCreary, 'Corrymeela—The Search for Peace'. Christian Journals Ltd., Belfast 1975.

[2] New Ulster Movement. Booklets (see Public Records Office, Belfast).

The Legal Basis of Partition in Ireland	1971
A Commentary on the Programme of Reforms for Northern Ireland	1971
The Reform of Stormont	1971
The Way Forward	1971
Northern Ireland and the Common Market	1972
Two Irelands or One?	1972
Violence and Northern Ireland	1972
A New Constitution for Northern Ireland	1972
Towards the Return of Rule of Law	1972
Tribalism or Christianity in Ireland	1973
What Price Independence?	1976

Chapter 7

[1] According to a Marplan Survey, made December 1967, for the *Belfast Telegraph* 16% of Catholics stated that the existing Stormont regime was 'the best

arrangement'. Professor Rose's survey (see Chapter 2) showed that 21% of Catholics wishes for 'no change' (Governing without Consensus', p.213). By 1978 according to E. P. Moxon-Browne's Queen's University Attitude Survey only 1% of Catholics wanted to see a return to the old Stormont regime, but by this time power-sharing had come upon the scene, and 39% of Catholics opted for a devolved government with power-sharing as the most acceptable solution. Only 25% of Catholics wanted the traditional Irish Unity with a break with Britain.

[2] Quoted by M. Wallace, 'Northern Ireland—50 years of self-government', p.77.

[3] Conor Cruise O'Brien, 'Ireland—can the Border be re-drawn?' *Observer*, 3 May and 7 June 1981.

[4] The figures are taken from the 1961 Census, the last Census where an answer regarding religious affiliation was obligatory. In the 1971 Census 9% of the population chose not to answer this question. The Catholic population officially dropped to 31.4%. Independent research was made by Dr. P. A. Compton, 'Northern Ireland: A Census Atlas', basing the study on the District Council area returns and applying the denominational breakdown of 1961 for the area to the proportion of the 9% not responding to the religious question. Dr. Compton estimated that the Catholic proportion in 1971 had risen to 36.8%.

[5] Quoted by J. Hunter. Background paper to Corrymeela/Glencree Conference on 'Models of Political Co-operation'. Held Queen's University, Belfast, March 1981.

[6] Quoted by J. A. Bristow. Ibid.

[7] 'Northern Ireland Problem', op. cit., p.108.

[8] 'Do we need a Bill of Rights?' Ed. C. Campbell. Based on contributions to a Conference arranged by the Standing Advisory Commission on Human Rights in Northern Ireland'. March 1981. Queen's University, Belfast.

[9] J. A. Bristow. Op. cit.

[10] Northern Ireland Attitude Survey. Queen's University. E. P. Moxon-Browne, op. cit.

[11] 'Northern Ireland Problem', op. cit., p.96.

[12] Ibid., pp.97-100, 120-125.
'Orange and Green', pp.20-24.
C. Hewitt, 'Catholic grievances, Catholic nationalism and violence in Northern Ireland during the Civil Rights Period'. *British Journal of Sociology*, Vol. XXXII, No. 3, Sept. 1981, pp.364-367.

[13] W. I. Jennings, 'A Federation for Western Europe', 1940, pp.61-64.
J. H. Whyte, 'The Reform of Stormont', June 1971. New Ulster Movement booklet.

[14] E. A. Aunger, 'In Search of Political Stability: a comparative study of New Brunswick and Northern Ireland'. McGill, 1981, pp.35-38, p.54.

[15] J. A. Oliver, 'Ulster To-day and To-morrow', P, E.P., Vol. XLIV, Broadsheet No. 576, March 1978.

[16] E. P. Moxon-Browne, op. cit. See Appendix B.

Appendices

A. CHRONOLOGICAL TABLE

Year	*Political event*		*Report*
1968			
5.10	Civil Rights March, Londonderry.		
22.11	Package deal of Reforms.		
1969			
Jan.	NUM and PACE formed.		
24.2	O'Neill election.		
28.4	**O'Neill resigns, Chichester-Clark PM.**		
13.8	Riots in Londonderry and Belfast.		
15.8	Army on streets.		
		12.9	Cameron Report.
		10.10	Hunt Report.
27.11	Ombudsman established.		
2.12	Community Relations Commission formed.		
1970			
11.1	Provisional IRA formed in Dublin.		
21.4	Alliance Party formed.		
4.7	Curfew on Lower Falls.		
21.8	SDLP formed.		
1971			
23.2	**Chichester-Clark resigns. W. B. Faulkner PM.**		
9.8	Internment reintroduced. Riots.		
		16.11	Compton Report.
1972			
30.1	Bloody Sunday, Londonderry; 13 killed.		
		9.2	Parker Committee Report.

Year	*Political event*		*Report*
30.3	**STORMONT PROROGUED, DIRECT RULE, W. Whitelaw Sec. of State.**		
		6.4	Scarman Tribunal Report.
		19.4	Widgery Report.
21.7	Bloody Friday, Belfast; 9 killed, 130 injured.		
31.7	End of 'no-go' areas. Bombs on Claudy; 8 killed.		
24.9	Darlington Conference.		
		20.12	Diplock Committee Report
1973			
8.3	Border Poll.		
2.4	Emergency Provisions Act.		
30.5	Local Government Elections for 26 Councils.		
28.6	Elections for Northern Ireland Assembly.		
Aug.	**NORTHERN IRELAND ASSEMBLY.**		
		31.10	Kilbrandon Report.
9.12	Sunningdale Meetings.		
1974			
1.1	Northern Ireland Executive in Office.		
28.2	Westminster Elections.		
5.3	**Merlyn Rees Secretary of State.**		
14.5	Ulster Workers' Strike commences.		
17.5	Bombs in Monaghan and Dublin; 28 killed.		
28.5	**NORTHERN IRELAND EXECUTIVE FALLS. Direct Rule re-established.**		
4.7	Proposals for Constitutional Convention.		
9.12	Feakle Talks. IRA Ceasefire over Christmas.		

Year	Political event		Report
1975			
10.1	IRA Ceasefire extended.	10.1	Gardiner Report.
1.5	Election for Constitution.		
7.11	Convention completed its work.		
Dec.	Internment without trial phased out.		
1976			
3.2	Convention reconvened.		
5.3	Convention finally dissolved.		
1.3	Ending of Special Category prisoners.		
14.8	Formation of Peace People. Marches: 28.8 Shankill Road. 21.10 Falls Road.		
10.8	**Roy Mason takes over from M. Rees as Secretary of State.**		
5.12	Peace People's Boyne March.		
1977			
3.4	B. Faulkner dies as a result of accident.		
2.5	Attempted second Workers' Strike collapses.		
19.5	Local Government Elections.		
10.8	Visit of Queen.		
1978			
Mar.	Commencement of 'dirty' protest at Maze prison.		
13.5	Amnesty International report on interrogation methods. Bennett Committee set up as a result.		
1979			
16.3	Bennett Committee reports on interrogation methods.		
May	**UK election. H. Atkins Secretary of State.**		
27.8	Earl Mountbatten murdered.		
29.9	Pope's visit to the Republic of Ireland.		

Year	Political event	Report
1980		
7.1	Atkins' initiative on devolution. Terminated end March.	
15.5	European Commission on Human Rights. Judgement on political status.	
21.5	First of Summit Meetings.	
Nov.	First series of hunger strikes commenced.	
8.12	Second Summit Meeting.	
Dec.	First series of hunger strikes called off.	
1981		
6.2	Paisley's 'Carson trail'.	
1.3	Second series of hunger strikes commenced.	
9.4	Fermanagh/South Tyrone By-Election. Bobby Sands elected.	
5.5	Bobby Sands died. Riots in Catholic areas.	
21.8	Fermanagh/South Tyrone second By-Election. Owen Carron elected.	
1.9	Lagan College. First integrated school.	
13.9	**J. Prior replaces H. Atkins as Secretary of State.**	
3.10	Hunger strike terminated.	
2.11	Third Summit Meeting.	
13.11	R. Bradford, MP, assassinated. Protestant demonstrations.	

B. NATIONAL IDENTITIES

Opinion Survey Professor Richard Rose 1968 'Governing without Consensus', p.208

Which of these terms describes the way you usually think of yourself?

	Protestant %	*Catholic* %	*Total* %
Irish	20	76	43
British	39	15	29
Ulsterman	32	5	21
Sometimes British / Sometimes Irish	6	3	5
Anglo-Irish	2	1	1
Don't Know	1	—	1

Queen's University Attitude Survey E. P. Moxon-Browne M.A. 1978.

Religious and National Identity

	Protestants %	*Catholics* %
Irish	7.8	69.1
British	66.8	15.2
Ulster	19.8	5.7

Survey awaiting publication.

C. SECURITY STATISTICS 1969 – 1981

	1969	*1970*	*1971*	*1972*	*1973*	*1974*	*1975*	*1976*	*1977*	*1978*	*1979*	*1980*	*1981*
KILLED													
Army/UDR	—	—	48	129	66	35	20	29	27	21	48	16	23
RUC/RUC Reserve	1	2	11	17	13	15	11	23	14	10	14	9	21
Civilians[1]	12	23	114	322	171	166	217	245	69	50	51	50	55
Total	13	25	173	468	250	216	248	297	110	81	113	75	99
Total road deaths	257	272	304	372	335	316	313	300	355	288	293	229	223
EXPLOSIVES													
Explosions	8	155	1022	1382	978	685	399	766	366	455	420	280	398
Explosions (in tons)[2]	NA	NA	4.9	22.1	22.1	20.7	6.2	7.6	1.0	2.6	2.0	2.9	4.1
Bombs diffused	—	—	493	471	542	428	236	426	169	178	142	120	132
Explosive found (in tons)	—	0.4	1.2	18.5	17.2	11.7	5.2	9.7	1.7	1.0	0.9	0.8	3.4
Firearms found	NA	NA	717	1264	1595	1260	825	837	590	400	301	203	398
ROBBERIES													
Numbers	—	NA	437	1931	1215	1231	1201	813	591	442	434	412	587
Amounts stolen (£000s)	—	NA	304	791	612	573	572	546	447	233	568	497	855
Charged with terrorist offences	—	—	—	531	1414	1362	1197	1276	1308	843	670	550	918

[1] This figure includes terrorists
[2] Estimated figures

Source: Hansard 11 February 1982, p.421-422
Ulster Handbooks

D SELECTED BIBLIOGRAPHY

HISTORICAL DEVELOPMENT

Beckett, J. C. — A Short History of Ireland. Hutchinson, 1952
The Making of Modern Ireland. Faber, 1962

Lyons, F. S. L. — Ireland since the Famine. Weidenfeld & Nicolson, 1971

Moody, T. W. — The Ulster Question 1603–1963. Mercier, 1974

Mansergh, P. N. S. — The Government of Northern Ireland: a study in devolution. G. Allen and Unwin, 1936
The Irish Question 1840–1921. G. Allen & Unwin, 1965

FACTS ON THE NORTHERN IRELAND GOVERNMENT

Flackes, W. D. — Northern Ireland: a Political Directory 1968–1979. Gill & MacMillan, 1980

Wallace, M. — Northern Ireland: 50 years of Self-Government. David & Charles, 1971

THE NATIONALIST CASE

Gallagher, F. — The Indivisible Ireland. Gollancz, 1957

THE REPUBLICAN POSITION

Coogan, T. P. — The IRA. Fontana Books (revision) 1980

Farrell, M. — Northern Ireland; the Orange State. Pluto Press, 1976

Devlin, B. — The Price of my Soul. Pan, 1969

THE PROTESTANT POSITION

Harbinson, J. — The Ulster Unionist Party. Blackstaff Press, 1973

Stewart, A. T. Q. — The Ulster Crisis. Faber, 1967
The Narrow Ground. Faber, 1977

ANALYSIS OF THE SITUATION

Barritt, D. P. and Carter, C. F. — The Northern Ireland Problem. Oxford University Press plus additional chapters to 1972. O.U.P., 1962

Barritt, D. P. and Booth, A. — Orange and Green. A Quaker study of community relations in Northern Ireland. Northern Friends Peace Board, 1972

Dalby, J. — Conflict in Northern Ireland: the development of a polarised community. Gill & MacMillan, 1976

Heslinga, M. W. — Irish Border as a Cultural Divide. Van Gorcum, 1962

Oliver, J. — Ulster To-Day and To-morrow. P.E.P., 1978

Rose, R. — Governing without Consensus. Faber, 1971

THE LEGAL SYSTEM

Boyle, K. Hadden, T. Hillyard — 'Ten Years on in Northern Ireland: the legal control of political violence'. Cobden Trust, 1980

Campbell, C. Ed. — 'Do we need a Bill of Rights?' Maurice Temple Smith, 1980

SOCIAL EFFECTS OF VIOLENCE

Darby, J. and Williamson, A. — Violence and the Social Services in Northern Ireland. Heinemann, 1978

Murphy, D. — A Place Apart. John Murray, 1978

SPECIAL ASPECTS

Aunger, E. A. — In Search of Political Stability: a comparative study of New Brunswick and Northern Ireland. McGill. Queen's University Press, 1981

Bleakley, D. — Faulkner—Conflict and Consent in Irish Politics. Mowbrays, 1974

Fisk, R. — The Point of No Return: The strike which broke the British in Ulster. Andre Deutsch, 1975

Harris, R. — Prejudice and Tolerance in Ulster. A study of neighbours and strangers in a border community. Manchester University Press, 1972

Joint Study Group Irish Council of Churches/Roman Catholic Hierarchy — Violence in Ireland: A report to the Churches. Christian Journals, 1976

Oliver, J. — Working at Stormont

Watt, D. ed. — The Constitution of Northern Ireland. Problems and Prospects. National Institute of Economic and Social Research. Policy Studies Institute. Royal Institute of International Affairs. Heinemann, 1981

Quaker Peace & Service is a department of the Religious Society of Friends (Quakers) in Great Britain and Ireland. It was founded in 1978 to combine the peace activity of Friends Peace & International Relations Committee with the international personal service of Friends Service Council.

Quaker Peace & Service works for non-violent change and reconciliation between individuals, groups and nations. It campaigns to reform or replace oppressive systems while giving on-the-spot help to the hungry, the sick, the refugees and the tortured. Its programmes include the witness against warfare of all kinds and the advancement of small-scale, self-help agricultural and medical projects in Africa and Asia.

The Northern Friends Peace Board, founded in 1913, is a representative organisation of the Religious Society of Friends in the north of Great Britain. Its work has been mainly concerned with disarmament, Northern Ireland, education for peace in the broadest sense, and the implementation of the Friends Peace Testimony today. It has recently taken major new initiatives in the field of East-West reconciliation and this area of work is expected to expand. It works at a variety of different levels: local, regional, national, and international. It is particularly interested in work with young people, and in taking the message of peace to those who have not heard it before.

NORTHERN IRELAND

Inset (left) shows the six-county state of Northern Ireland, plus Cavan, Monaghan and Donegal, once part of the nine-county Province of Ulster.

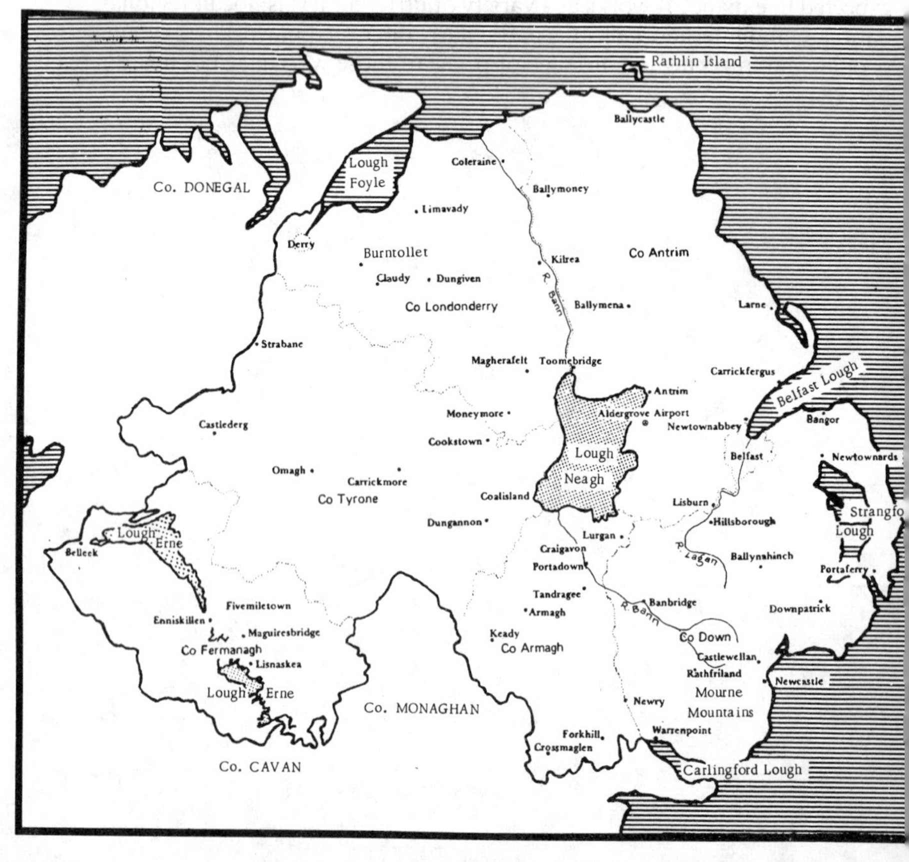